ALL ABOUT CHANGE

ALL ABOUT CHANGE

How to Successfully Make
Personal Life Changes

Sarah Carter

NEW DEGREE PRESS

ALL ABOUT CHANGE

How to Successfully Make Personal Life Changes

ISBN

978-1-63730-829-5 *Paperback*

978-1-63730-891-2 *Kindle Ebook*

978-1-63730-959-9 *Digital Ebook*

To my grandfather:

I know you'd be proud of this.

CONTENTS

INTRODUCTION

——

#TakeChargeOfYourChange

Change is a daily topic of conversation in all of our lives. Reflect on the conversations you've had this week. How many times did you use the word change? How many different contexts did you use it in? Change your mind. Change your clothes. Change a diaper (at least ten times a day in my house currently). Change your work-out routine. Change your address. Change your boss. There are *thirty one* entries for the word "change" in the *Merriam-Webster Dictionary*—two main entries along with twenty-nine subentries. We use the word change *a lot* and in many different contexts.

A common context people tend to use the word change in is with emotionally negative sayings about change that we've all heard. Change is inevitable. You can't control change. Change is the one constant in life. Change is scary. These sayings set the mental stage for change to be challenging, forced, and wild.

Then, when you do a quick internet search of "What do people think about change," you get results in three generalized themes. These themes may be frustrating because they seem not to relate to you and the type of change you are undergoing.

Search Themes:

1. Corporate Related: Results about how leaders and organizations make changes, which don't seem to apply to personal change at all. For example, one of the first search results is an article from *Forbes* that initially looks like it might take a personal approach from the wording of the title, "The big reason why some people are terrified of change (while others love it)." Then you read the first sentence, and nope, it's an article about change through the lens of the workplace (Murphy, 2016).

2. 10-Step Programs: Lists of tips and tricks on how to go about changing habits and/or behaviors in your life for everything from traveling to losing weight to starting over in a new relationship to investing your money.

3. Articles asking "Why?": Why do people resist change? Why is change so hard? Why can't I make this change? Why do people struggle to change? There are endless articles that blend together, as they all play on the same emotions.

The common phrases we've heard and the thousands of internet search results all paint change in a negative light. You either get tips and tricks that should help you because you haven't managed to succeed yet on your own or you get negative questions that make your change seem even more hopeless. No wonder people have a negative mindset about change and they try to resist it every time a change comes their way!

What if we thought of change differently? What if instead of thinking, "Change is scary, and I can't control it, so I'm going to avoid and resist it," we thought, "I have an opportunity for change! What can I do to harness it and use it to bring more success and joy into my life?" My friend Kimberly told me this improved pattern of thinking is how she approached the changes her circumstances brought her, though she didn't start out thinking this way.

Kimberly's childhood home wasn't far from where she decided to go to college, but it might as well have been on the moon because she'd never left home before for any extended period of time. She left early for school so she could work at the student bookstore, and she went home every weekend and every holiday. It was her routine, and it never changed. She was a classic homebody who liked the certainty of her lifestyle. Then one weekend during her freshman year, her routine changed. Her parents went out of town, and they told her she couldn't go home. They told her she had to step out of her comfort zone and stay on campus.

After the initial shock of her routine being disrupted, Kimberly embraced it as an opportunity. She got to see and experience aspects of campus life she hadn't up to that point. She spent time with friends outside of class and studying. She used school resources she didn't have time to use during the week. She also saw parts of the college town she hadn't seen before. Kimberly enjoyed her new routine so much she didn't go home again until Christmas (much to her mom's surprise). She had tunnel vision and fear, like many of us do when we are experiencing new situations, that held her to her comfortable routine. Once Kimberly decided to treat change as an adventurous opportunity for growth, she was hooked on treating change as an opportunity in all arenas of her life.

Kimberly became a real estate agent soon after graduation. She took all the necessary exams and joined an agency in a town where she knew no one and did not know the market. Everything was going really well, but just a few years later, she started to feel burnt out and uninspired. She told herself it was a normal feeling everyone experienced once they were truly settled into a job, and she didn't think much of it.

Then one day, Kimberly went to a bookstore. She went seeking a book with a remedy for her recurring burnt-out feeling, and a book title caught her eye. She read the description on the back to see if it could help her situation. The description mentioned being a coach. This sparked a thought that captured her attention: "What would it be like to be a coach instead of a real estate agent?" This thought ignited some much-needed inspiration and creativity for her to ponder. She told me she began to wonder about that change, and she kept circling back to that thought over the course of the next few years.

Five years passed. Kimberly was still selling real estate, making good money, and enjoying the routine that spoke to her homebody roots. She took a real estate training course with a company in California that she really enjoyed. She later heard that same company had created a real estate agent coaching program. The training company had seen how impactful business coaching could be and thought a tailored coaching experience for real estate agents could boost their effectiveness and give them an edge over their competitors. The word coach rang out to Kimberly, and she decided to sign up to be coached, which ultimately led to her being offered a coaching position.

Kimberly didn't hesitate at the opportunity to change course by becoming a coach for real estate agents. She experienced the coaching firsthand as a part of her training, then she began the training to become a coach for others. She set and achieved several goals along the way, and now twenty years later, she's still coaching and loving it! She credits her "harness-the-opportunity" approach for her success and happiness over that time. "I did not hesitate, and I did it afraid," she told me in our interview after conveying her story.

Kimberly's enthusiasm and positivity surrounding her approach to change is energizing. She's up for trying anything and everything because she strives to see all change, big or small, as an opportunity. This doesn't mean it's easy. She still has to work through it, and she is still afraid every now and then. "If you're doing something big, there will naturally be some trepidation. You'll never get to a place where you are totally comfortable with change," said Kimberly. There will always be a level of challenge.

Change doesn't have to be drastic, scary, or dramatically life changing. It is a natural part of a successful, well-lived life. You also don't have to be a celebrity, CEO, or have thousands of followers on social media for your change to be important and/or hard. We all go through change, and we can all learn something from others, even our friendly, hometown real estate agent coach.

I believe too many people resist changes in their lives because they go into it feeling like they have no control over it and there's no hope of making it successfully. This perpetuates the "resist mindset," and then they get stuck in a negative cycle, never fully making the change. It's a fallacy, though. Change is an opportunity to be harnessed! There is hope for change with the right mindset.

Successful change is a skill set. There are pieces and parts to it you can hone over time so you will be happier and more successful with each change you harness. In the chapters to come, I'll tell you about some skills you can use. Some of these skills and processes may sound familiar—setting goals, networking, having an accountability partner, and more. I'm a big believer in learning from trailblazers. Awesome people who came before me identified many of the key pieces to successful change. What will be different in this book than those before it is how I'll tie all of those skills together. I will link these highly effective skills into a mental playbook you can lean on every time an opportunity for change presents itself in your life. Now that you have this playbook, all you have to do is practice and implement—and you can start right now with any change you are facing.

The skills aren't the only pieces linked together in this book. I also want you to realize life changes aren't stand-alone events. You will make dozens of major and minor changes over the course of your life that, if done mindfully, will lead you to who you ultimately want to become. Each time a change opportunity comes up, it is also an opportunity to shape your ultimate reality, or as I like to call it, your living room when you're eighty.

I decided to write this book because the process of change fascinates me. I've undergone so many changes I sometimes identify as a chameleon. Change has taken me from small town island girl to big city living in New Orleans, then later from a military academy student delivering cargo around the world by ship to flying Navy P-8/A Poseidons (a military version of the most common commercial airplane used around the world—the 737—so if you've ever flown, you've probably ridden on one). Though I have worked to harness all of my changes, I know others who've had the same opportunities who have not navigated their courses as successfully. I began wondering why my methods yielded results consistent with my objectives. I put my coaching mind to work, asking big questions to unravel the differences between my process and that of others.

I'll be presenting some of the questions that guided my exploration throughout each chapter. I encourage you to reflect on these with an open and honest mind. No one is grading your answers to the questions, and unless you tell someone, no one is even going to know you thought about them. Look at these questions as your personal pathway to self-development so you can fully examine any change you're going through or thinking about making. Though some of the verbiage may seem corporate, you do not have view change from a career perspective for this book to apply to you. Substitute the language that applies best to your unique change in those instances so the question resonates authentically with you.

Harnessing change as an opportunity, like I learned to and like Kimberly did, involves a growth mindset along with tangible skills and processes to ensure you stay the course. Hearing stories of others that can serve as motivation and encouragement is another key to success when change is involved. The stories in this book are of regular people who've walked through changes that should feel relatable to you. This was really important to me. I want these stories to sound like what you or someone you know have gone through. No millionaire TikTok stars here. (Okay, maybe a couple celebrity appearances because who doesn't love a good pop culture reference?) Though some names have been shortened or changed to protect privacy, the majority of the people these vignettes will introduce you to are my friends, family members, neighbors, school mates, and people of my community. I'm sharing their stories here to inspire you to take charge of your change and become the most genuine version of yourself you can envision.

If you're going through a job transition, shifting family dynamic, if you're moving, starting/stopping/restarting school, beginning a new sport, lifestyle, or anything in between, this book and the harnessing change approach therein will positively impact your journey. Take encouragement from all of these stories and use them to build your change skills. Store the lessons they reveal and draw from those the next time you encounter a change that seems intimidating at first. Spend some time with the questions I'll present throughout the chapters to order your steps and make sure you're digging into the root of your decisions. With these examples, skills, and questions in your tool kit, you'll see your next change as an opportunity to be your most successful one yet.

PART 1

HOW WE
GOT HERE

CHAPTER 1

WHY WE RESIST CHANGE

———

I have a big fear of change, or
negative change, anyway.

—KELLY CLARKSON

Close your eyes, open all of your senses, and imagine popping the tab to a bubbly, crisp, sweet Coca-Cola. Hear the sound of the small burst of pressurized air rushing free, feel your hand gripping the chilled iconic red and white can as you bring it to your lips for a big gulp on a hot summer day. Ahhhhhhh . . . refreshing. You probably didn't even pay much attention to the act of purchasing this can. You know exactly what it looks like after years of seeing it in the vending machine lineup, the cooler section of the store, or in the bright red cardboard box in the soda aisle. I bet if I asked you, you could draw it from memory. At least, you could have drawn it, until one day during the fall of 2011 when it all briefly changed.

Where did the red can go? What is this new, polar bear white can all about? Is it the same Coca-Cola? Or is it something new? What was wrong with the old stuff? How could they do this to me, change my Coca-Cola experience out of the blue?

Turmoil in the stores and ferocious pushback on the internet gripped the United States when Coca-Cola rolled out what the marketing team believed would be a well-received holiday-themed color scheme update. "It was the first time in 125 years that Coke changed its can color. And it didn't go over too well," read a headline in *Time* magazine (Carbone, 2011).

It didn't go over well because the majority of people's initial reaction to any change will be resistance. We have all been conditioned over years of seeing and experiencing Coca-Cola as a red can to know what to expect when we take that first sip. Thanks to modern, repeatable manufacturing processes, you know for certain what it will taste like, smell like, how it will make you feel, and exactly how long it will take you to drink the entire can. You control that experience, and it feels safe. Our brains have evolved to like safety and certainty. We like these two feelings so much we strive to recreate them as often as possible. According to neuroscientists Derler and Ray in *Why Change Is So Hard—and How to Deal With It*, this process of recreating safety and certainty allows us to control our environments and have more predictability in our daily lives.

Change does not feel safe. Any change, great or small, lacks certainty. No matter how hard you work to instill certainty into any change, there will always be a level of unpredictability. The marketing team at Coca-Cola undoubtedly worked to envision every possible outcome for the launch of their white cans, but they failed to predict the consumer's neurological response.

Our initial resistant response often outwardly manifests itself in negative emotions or negative statements like the ones we've all heard before such as: Change is scary. Change is hard. You can't control change, and many more statements. "We tell ourselves that the change will be *difficult* (hard to do, complicated, awkward), *costly* (time-consuming, damaging to us or our reputation), and/or *weird* (not how people act, not what's expected). When we tell ourselves these things, it makes the change seem foolish or even dangerous . . . It automatically sets us up to resist or even sabotage the change" (Andersen, 2019). Rumors erupted nearly instantaneously about the liquid in the white Coca-Cola cans. It must be a new recipe the company was experimenting with, and the original, time-honored, beloved version was gone forever. *Gasp!* Stress and fear gripped consumers. Coca-Cola received so many negative, resistant, anxious comments that the white cans were recalled and the whole marketing plan was scrapped in just one month.

> *Coaching Question: Think about the nature of a change you are going through (i.e., new job, back to work, school, retirement, family dynamic change, etc.). Picture yourself there, in the new role. Imagine all the minute details down to colors, smells, and feel of the new desk chair, car, home, country, and so on. Doing this will help you consider any areas where you feel a lack of safety and certainty. With these identified, you can work to overcome those feelings.*

STRESS-FEAR-ANXIETY CYCLE

Think about a time you were on your way to your local grocery store, office, child's school, favorite restaurant, or some other routine place and you encountered a detour in your typical route. What was your immediate reaction? Was it something akin to, "Well shoot, how long will this set me back? Where the heck will this take me? Is this going to be a permanent thing? Uuuugh." We've all been there and thought those kinds of thoughts about changes of all sizes. Change, whether it's anticipated or not, can initially appear to be inconvenient, frustrating, time-consuming, and several other negative adjectives.

Unexpected changes filled with uncertainty are notorious for igniting a resistance mindset, but anticipated change can seem just as challenging. I vividly remember the day I moved out of my college dorm room (we called them barracks rooms because of the military lingo we applied to every aspect of our lives at the US Merchant Marine Academy). My 2004 gunmetal gray Mustang was loaded to the point of bulging at the door seams with all of my worldly possessions, and my room was bare. I did four or five final checks of all the drawers, the wardrobe, under the bed, under the mattress, behind the door, and everywhere else before continuing to delay my exit by standing on the threshold, paralyzed by the thought of leaving.

It was over. I was standing at the edge of what felt like a bottomless crevasse between my known, comfortable college life and the next big step that would usher me into the rest of my life. I'd planned for the day I'd move on from college. I'd done my best to anticipate all of the fear-inducing uncertainty. I'd worked through all the good processes and asked all the big questions to make sure I'd set myself up for success. Still, I was immobilized. The stress, fear, and anxiety of the unknown in my mind at that moment had me feeling unsafe and overwhelmed.

This was a huge change, and despite spending literally years preparing for the day I would put college in my rearview mirror for the last time, I was frozen. Would I fit in as a Naval Officer? The piece of paper I received with my US Merchant Marine Academy diploma commissioning me as an officer said I was qualified, but would I *fit in*? Would I make the cut to be a pilot? I'd passed the initial test, but that's just the first hurdle! Would I be any good at flying? Had I done enough training to not look foolish on day one? I was succumbing to the classic cycle of stress and fear created by a lack of certainty and safety.

All changes, great and small, are stressful and have the potential to produce a vicious stress and fear cycle. Tonja Blom and Rica Viljoen of the University of South Africa and University of Reading, respectively, presented their findings on how humans react to change at a conference in 2016. In it, they describe this hallmark pitfall to change in the most succinct way I've heard: "Stress creates fear, which creates more stress, which then creates anxiety and resistance, which again results in increased fear and stress. This stress, anxiety, fear, and resistance cycle is fueled by the individual's away responses" (Blom & Viljoen, 2016).

Coaching Question: Is the change you are making one that you chose? If not, how can you frame it in a positive light to help reduce the stress-fear-anxiety cycle? Writing it down in a positive way and committing to viewing it in this new light will give you back some control of this process.

YOUR BRAIN ON CHANGE

The Partnership for a Drug-Free America ran a public service announcement (PSA) campaign in the late 1980s and into the 1990s called "Frying Pan." A man shows you a regular, white breakfast egg, stating, "This is your brain." He then motions to a large, empty frying pan. As he says, "This is your brain on drugs," he cracks the egg into the pan where it then begins to congeal and cook. This PSA was hailed by *TV Guide* as one of the top one hundred commercials of all time. It simply explained how your brain reacts to illicit substances, and the ad has spawned several spin-offs and parodies, ensuring its lesson endures (Alexander, 2000).

Similarly, your brain on change is a liquid mess. Maybe not to full fried breakfast egg consistency, as demonstrated in the "Frying Pan" PSA, but at least a sunny-side up version. As previously discussed, your brain will more often than not perceive change as a stressor. This triggers your amygdala—the lizard part of your brain that has yet to evolve fully and determines your emotions. Your amygdala interprets the outside stimulation signal and delivers its assessment to the hypothalamus (Harvard Health, 2020). The hypothalamus is a bit like a recorded phone menu of options that controls your central nervous system. It has scripted responses depending on what signal is sent to it from your amygdala.

Change is a stressor. So when your amygdala is stimulated by impending change, it tells the hypothalamus you are in distress. The hypothalamus reacts according to its scripted auto-response list like the good little recorded menu it is. Its first action is to flood your body with adrenaline like the egg dropping into the hot pan. This will cause several physical changes to your body (elevated heart rate, increased blood pressure, sweating, and increased breathing, to name a few). All of these physical changes are uncomfortable, so of course, you want to resist them and get out of it as soon as possible. Meanwhile, your thinking is altered too. You become hyper focused on what caused so much stress. You can't work through any other problems that come your way while in this state of adrenaline-fueled cooking. You can train your brain to react differently. Over time, your body can recognize change as an opportunity to harness and use the change to propel you forward *toward* who you want to be instead of *away* from the stress and perceived threat.

> *Coaching Question: When have you felt this state of intense stress? Identify all the physical and emotional feelings you had in that state of stress. Are you feeling any of those now, or do you foresee the potential for them as you are thinking about the change you are making or will make?*

AWAY AND TOWARD

The Coca-Cola can, an unexpected detour, and leaving college probably sound like small changes, totally easy to accept and move past. You may be wondering, "Sure, but what about the really hard, out-of-the-blue stuff like losing my job or suddenly having to take care of a loved one?" Both of those scenarios are indeed initially much scarier and will challenge your amygdala. My friend Harriet once found herself facing both of those big changes within months of each other.

All Harriet could hear was beeping. The doctor was standing right in front of her describing the past six hours of surgical procedures in detail. She could see the doctor's lips moving, but she heard nothing except the beeping. Her husband of forty years was lying in a hospital bed six feet away, cut open from throat to belly button. From where they were standing, she could see the nearly three-foot-long incision, only loosely closed with plastic wrap just in case they needed to "jump back in to massage his heart" again.

Harriet knew Mike had a major cardiac episode. She knew he was alive only because of the more than a dozen machines that had to keep beeping. She also knew her life was going to change because of all of it. She started to make out snippets of the statements the doctors and nurses said over the next few hours: heart pump, left ventricular assist device (LVAD), heart transplant, waiting list, rehabilitation. Her vocabulary expanded to include all the new terms, and her mind began to form a loose timeline. The beeping, though, it blared loudest and kept her in a semi-constant state of being overwhelmed and resistant. "I just want to go home and come back and have everything back to normal," she told me in the cold, hushed cardiac ward's waiting room over lukewarm coffee and generic turkey sandwiches from the cafeteria.

Their lives will never go back to normal. This "out-of-the-blue change" upended their routine and forced them to create a new normal. Like most of us do when confronted with spontaneous, unwanted change, they resisted it. Harriet tried to go back to work. Mike tried to recover by himself at home. It became clear after a few weeks and a couple of panicked calls from Mike to Harriet's work while he was waiting on an ambulance to pick him up that their pre-event normal would no longer work. Harriet needed to make two difficult, big changes. She needed to quit her job, and she needed to become Mike's caregiver, at least until the initial aftereffects of Mike's new normal had become routine and manageable.

The overwhelming senses of frustration, defeat, and fear all balled up into one messy clump of emotions in Harriet's stomach. This was not a change she'd ever foreseen. She loved working. The sense of purpose and accomplishment she derived from it put a smile on her face just thinking about it. She tried to think of any way she could continue to work and be Mike's caregiver at the same time but came up empty.

She told me, "Acceptance was the hardest part," but once she overcame that, she was able to put the puzzle together. She was able to see the positives this could lead to, like more time together and more time with other family members, home improvement projects they'd been meaning to do, and other small life-improving changes like diet, exercise, and hobbies. Once she'd moved past the fear, the silver lining started to shine.

Harriet naturally resisted these big life changes. Who could blame her? Watching your loved one go through such an enormous trauma is enough to make anyone step back in shocked fear. Having the ripple effects of that change dictate the life you'd worked so hard to establish and leaned on for meaning and direction is distressing even to imagine. Harriet's initial reaction was wanting to physically move away from the change by going home, a familiar place. Resisting change is the mind's method of attempting to move you away from the perceived threat. I can imagine anyone in a similar situation to Harriet's would feel the ball of emotions that she did and resist their change. We resist change, especially if we don't feel in control.

Does it have to be like this? Does your first reaction to change have to be a resisting, away response, or is a better way of approaching change available to you? Can you move toward changes in your life to make them positive experiences? Absolutely! Blom and Viljoen, who detailed the stress-fear-anxiety cycle, also describe "away" and "toward" responses in their research. "Away responses" are what come from the resistance reaction most people initially have about change, whereas "toward responses" come from positive reactions and what I call a harnessing change approach (Blom & Viljoen, 2016). This harnessing approach is how people skip the stress cycle, make successful changes in their lives, and increase their happiness about the path before them.

Harriet eventually started to use the harnessing approach tools she'd learned from previous life changes to chart her journey through this new life change of being a full-time caregiver. She started to ask big questions, set goals, lean on her network for the support she needed, and take an active role so she had a sense of control in the whirlwind. Today Harriet is an active gardener, has tackled most of her home projects list, does light office work on occasion, and continues to approach the new changes life brings her with a "toward" response.

The skills Harriet found critical, and many more, are the focus of part two of this book! Through several more stories, you'll learn these skills and how they can help you successfully harness change in your life. The key to having a "toward" response and mastering the harnessing change approach is a growth mindset. So, before we dive into how to retrain your lizard brain and the skills you'll need, let's first examine what a growth mindset means and why you should have one.

Coaching Question: What are the other changes that have to take place alongside your main change (like Harriett having to leave her job)? Most changes come in sets. Thinking through them early will encourage your brain to choose a harnessing approach.

CHAPTER 2

GROWTH MINDSET

———

Life isn't about finding yourself. Life is about creating yourself.

—GEORGE BERNARD SHAW

My senior year of high school I played the center position on my basketball team. You know, the tall player. I am five feet four inches (1.63 m) tall. I'm not exactly a—ahem—natural fit for that position typically played by people likes Shaquille "Shaq" O'Neal, Candace Parker, and Lisa Leslie, who are all well over six feet (1.82 m) tall. A coach jokingly told me once that maybe if I just had a growth mindset, I'd be the perfect center. Clearly it was a joke and completely out of context.

You've probably also heard the term growth mindset used in any number of contexts. I've heard people use it when encouraging others to think outside the box, look at the positive side of some challenging situation, see the good that could come out of a failure, and many other instances. It always goes something like this: "I need you to go into this situation with a growth mindset, see what will come from this unique opportunity." This feels like speaking with the stereotypical used car salesman. They try to make the old junker sound like a brand-new sports car. You don't need to ask any questions to know they are trying to sell you a lemon. Nothing in that phrasing inspires positivity, and it certainly doesn't make "having a growth mindset" sound like a beneficial idea.

Carol Dweck, PhD, developed the term growth mindset and its tenets through years of research on how people cope with failure. Dr. Dweck's revolutionary work identifying the differences between growth mindset and its opposite, fixed mindset, has become so popular the terms have taken on altered meanings. These terms have become so overused and commercialized their originally intended meanings are largely lost. "People often confuse a growth mindset with being flexible or open-minded, or with having a positive outlook—qualities they believe they've simply always had . . . I call this a 'false growth mindset,'" Dweck clarifies in the *Harvard Business Review* article "What Having a 'Growth Mindset' Actually Means."

Dr. Dweck meant for people to approach new challenges and opportunities by asking, "How can I improve myself?" She states, "Individuals who believe their talents can be developed (through hard work, good strategies, and input from others) have a growth mindset" (Dweck, 2016). A growth mindset is about growing oneself—growing your knowledge, network, skills, and other attributes. This is the mindset and approach one must take to harness change as an opportunity.

"Growth mindset is based on the belief your basic qualities are things you can cultivate through your efforts . . . Everyone can change and grow through application and experience" (Dweck, 2016). According to Dr. Dweck, the opposite of a growth mindset is a fixed mindset. This is when you believe your skills, intelligence, and other qualities are stuck.

A person with a fixed mindset believes they were brought into the world with a certain amount of capacity for something and they will leave this world with the same amount of that something. No matter what they do, how much they study, or how many times they practice, it will always remain the same. A fixed mindset is made even more problematic because it drives the individual who assumes they are limited to avoid challenging situations that do not leverage their strengths or situations where their lack of skill may be revealed.

Change is inherently challenging. It will push you outside your typical skill sets and comfort zones. Approaching change with resistance is approaching change from a fixed mindset. You are assuming you have a fixed set of skills or intelligence regarding your situation. You feel the change you're facing would take you out of that skill and intelligence set, so you resist it.

On the other hand, by deciding to harness your change, you are taking a growth mindset approach. You are looking at it from the point of view of asking yourself "What can I learn from this?" With enough effort, some vision, and good strategy with skills honed over time, you'll become good at change. You will no longer look at it from a fixed mindset point of view.

Coaching Question: What mindset have you approached changes with in the past? Growth? Fixed? Or a mix of both?

VISION

I spoke with a former colleague, Saibatu Mansaray. She is one of the most inspiring people with whom I have ever had the pleasure of working. I wanted to know about her experience with growth mindset, as it has seemingly been her approach to many aspects of her life. It would have been easy for Saibatu to look at the hand she'd been dealt in life and decide, "This is it. This is the best I can do. I'm fixed." Many others around her in her childhood had taken that fixed mindset approach, and they seemed to be doing alright. Saibatu's father encouraged her throughout her youth to want more than alright.

Saibatu realized she wasn't initially going to find what her father was encouraging her toward in her homeland of Sierra Leone. She searched for a female role model who was striving to improve their situation, and she didn't find one. Faced with no other alternative, she left for a land she'd heard of that could give her endless opportunities: America.

She didn't just believe her skills and intelligence weren't fixed, Saibatu believed neither were those of her countrymen. She didn't leave Sierra Leone planning to never return. She left envisioning, "One day, I'll come back with the skills I've gained and do good here." First, she had to change herself. She had to become the role model she had needed but didn't find.

Saibatu's growth mindset approach to life led her to join the US Army and take advantage of all the schooling the Army would pay for. She became a physician assistant. During her twenty-three years of military service, she tended the wounds of fellow service members from the deserts of Iraq to the halls of the White House. The experiences she gained, the skills she cultivated, and the changes she chose all shaped who she has become.

Today, she is working in her home country of Sierra Leone. She strives to empower and inspire people to own their situation and bring change where necessary. She does this through her nonprofit organization, The Mansaray Foundation, and her podcasting project, *The Saibatu Mansaray Journey.* "I want [this] country, and continent, to dig deep and use [their] critical thinking and innovation" to change and evolve. She wants people to abandon the donor-driven, neocolonialism mindset that theorizes, "the only way I can be like America or anywhere else is if they give it to me." This is an outdated, fixed mindset approach. She wants them to see they "have the ability. We are the most intellectual, knowledgeable creatures that God created, and sometimes we just need a little push" to change mindsets and approaches.

During our talk, Saibatu told me about a village that only had one wooden crib in its clinic for all patients who were children—newborn to toddlers. She looked around the village and found a carpenter. "I said, 'You're a carpenter; that's made of wood. Can't you make it?' and that's when the mindset shifted." The whole village had been stuck with one crib in a fixed mindset. They thought they had to have more cribs given to them rather than try to fabricate more of their own.

They had the skilled labor available to them the whole time, but they lacked vision. That's the difference in approaching a challenging change with a growth mindset as opposed to a fixed mindset.

I'm not saying that in order to have a growth mindset, you have to want to bring big change to an entire country! Saibatu is an inspiring visionary, and she is making headway in her country. Your aim should initially be to have the vision the carpenter gained from their encounter with Saibatu. See the change you are facing as an opportunity to grow your existing skills. If shifting your mindset to one of growth for this current change you are facing leads you to want to do something huge, like Saibatu, then more power to you.

Coaching Question: Which approach, growth or fixed, comes more naturally to you?

NEUROPLASTICITY

Leveraging a growth mindset approach to change, even just once, sets you up to approach the next change the same way because of your brain's ability to evolve. Dr. Jordan Grafman has done a lot of research on the brain's ability to rewire functionality after it sustains an injury. His research identifies four types of neuroplasticity that are active in perfectly healthy people as well as those who have been injured.

One of the types of neuroplasticity Dr. Grafman identifies is "map expansion" (Grafman, 2000). This is how your brain absorbs a new skill like how to throw a curveball, play the twelve-string guitar, or think about new subject matter, such as differential equations or navigating a new grocery store. The area of your brain that will be dedicated to this skill will first expand to reorganize all the new information and processes. Over time and with repeated exposure, this skill becomes routine. Your brain standardizes the processes, and the region in the brain will return to its original size *but* with reorganized information.

Change is a skill we begin learning from childhood. Your brain creates a space dedicated to change processes from the moment you first encounter change. If your brain initially built fixed mindset processes and responses to change, then the first time you approach change from a growth mindset, your brain will begin to rewire. The region in your brain that stores your responses to change will begin to expand. This region in your brain will stay expanded as you continue to exercise your new skills and approach. This expansion allows new connections to be formed, rewiring and evolving what response functions you had previously stored.

The fixed mindset responses in your brain will be replaced with growth mindset responses with repeated use. Gradually, as you respond to more and more changes from a growth mindset approach, the region of your brain storing your change responses will return to its original size. The new connections made will be permanent, though, allowing for continued growth potential.

There is a proverbial carpenter in every village Saibatu visits. She witnesses aha moments like the crib regularly. These are the seeds of neuroplasticity map expansion. "People can't control all the things that happen to them. I can't control that I grew up in a country like this, but I can make sure it doesn't keep me from achieving my goals." Her experiences and her presence in the lives of the villages she works with spark change. She shows people, *her* people, a growth mindset approach can be successful. Seeing this jump-starts their brains into map expansion mode, and they begin to see the change she is bringing as the opportunity that it is.

"How are you received?" I asked her. She had been gone from Sierra Leone for over twenty-six years prior to our interview. I believed her absence from her home country for so long may have resulted in her countrymen labeling her an outsider. If that were the case, her efforts would have been met with a lot of resistance. "I have been received very well . . . People say 'No one does this. No one comes back, so thank you.'" The people she meets see that she has been successful in bringing change into her own life so they are willing to accept her and her approach to change in the hopes it will produce the same kinds of results for them.

> *Coaching Question: Have you experienced an aha moment where you could almost feel the brain expansion happen and the neuroplasticity process beginning?*

QUITTING AND FAILURE

Basketball was as much a part of me as my hair color. Ever since I could hold a little basketball-painted golf ball, I have loved the sport. If I wasn't playing, I was studying everything there was to know about it. My favorite team was the Orlando Magic. Shaq's height, incredible skill, and lively character consistently held my attention game after game. As I said earlier, my height doesn't allow me to tower over anyone except our family dog, but I loved watching Shaq dominate on the court. I dreamed of being a star college basketball player. The first step was choosing a college of course, so I had my parents take me to dozens of schools, starting with the smallest Division I school at the time: University of Wyoming.

The starting five Wyoming players greeted me when I checked in at the athletic director's office. What a rude awakening! The shortest one was five feet seven inches (1.70 cm) tall. I knew I could play with the best, but was that kind of challenge—playing with people who had an immediate advantage of at least three inches (7.6 cm) in both height and reach—worth it? Undeterred, we plodded along, visiting schools and meeting with a couple of scouts that came to my games. One of the scouts was a basketball coach from a school I had never heard of: the US Merchant Marine Academy (USMMA). He and I got along right from the start, and I scheduled a school visit before he got back on his plane to New York.

Less than a year later, I stepped onto the gym floor at the USMMA for the first time and was greeted by the same eager coach who'd seen me play down in New Orleans. His coaching approach was totally different from my high school coach, but not in a way I'd expected. My high school coach had been demanding, loud, animated, and intimidating when she showed you the correct position after you messed up a drill in practice. This man was quiet and let the team captains run the show, only stepping in when there seemed to be confusion.

The captains were another story. They were loud, but in a superior way. They didn't leave our hierarchical, military-based school life at the door. They still insisted we treat them as "higher ranking" upperclassmen—calling them ma'am rather than by their names—in every encounter except on the court for games. After five weeks, I'd had enough, but I didn't know what to do.

I'm not a quitter. I couldn't even put the words "I want to quit basketball" together in my brain without wanting to vomit. I not only felt like a quitter, but I felt like a failure because I'd made a commitment. That commitment was to the coach, to myself, and to some extent, to my parents to play. I needed to change but was stuck because there was something about basketball I wasn't ready to let go of yet.

I took a weekend and all but locked myself in my room to dedicate time to think through the situation. After two days, and very little sleep, the truth finally dawned on me. It wasn't basketball I wanted; it was to be a college athlete so I could have that experience in my life! This realization opened my eyes to sports I'd never heard of or considered, and it led me to explore the water-borne sports (which was something you'd think I'd have already done, given the school was training me to operate huge ocean-going ships). I joined the rowing team and became a coxswain for the men's team and had four full years of being a college athlete.

No one hits every foul shot, plays flawlessly through Beethoven, or effortlessly makes a big life change on their first try. You're going to brick a few shots, miss a note or two, and forget to close out the power bill before leaving your first apartment. These are unavoidable failures in a lifetime of changes. But "Failure is a friend. Failure is a learning tool.

Failure is a way to work yourself out of a bad situation and be better for the next situation," says Saibatu. She sees where villages have tried to change but stopped at the first fail. You have to keep going.

Dr. Dweck calls this the "power of yet," and it is part of the growth mindset. Her research included the study of children to whom she gave cognitive puzzles (Dweck, 2016). These puzzles were slightly too difficult for each child's age group. Dr. Dweck wasn't seeing how many children could manage to solve the puzzles. She was looking for their reactions to the difficulty of the puzzles. Those with a growth mindset saw their failure as an indication of their current limitations. These children treated the difficult puzzles as an opportunity to grow in the area of their current weaknesses and turn it into a strength.

Those children with a fixed mindset saw their inability to solve the puzzle just as failure. They quietly hoped they didn't look stupid because of it. "The passion for stretching yourself and sticking to it, even (or especially) when it's not going well, is the hallmark of the growth mindset" (Dweck, 2016).

Charles Manz wrote *The Power of Failure: 27 Ways to Turn Life's Setbacks into Success.* In it, he points out a poignant truth about failure and the role it plays in growth: "It is very often a misperception about the difference between what exists and what goes unnoticed (such as growth and learning when we fall short of reaching a goal) and what is realized later (longer term success)" (Manz, 2002). Without failure, there is no growth. Without continuing to try and learn, there is no brain map expansion. Without viewing the act of harnessing change as an opportunity and a skill you can hone, you will be stuck in a fixed mindset with a resistance attitude, but you will never quit or fail because you didn't try.

Coaching Question: When have you failed during a change? What did it look like, how did it feel, and how did it affect your approach to change the next time?

CHAPTER 3

WHY NOW?

———

You gain strength, courage, and confidence
by every experience in which you
really stop to look fear in the face.

—ELEANOR ROOSEVELT

Fire tornadoes. Record breaking snowfall. Murder hornets. Unprecedented police shootings. American unemployment levels unseen since the Great Depression. A hurricane season that ran out of letters in the alphabet. It's hard to believe all of those events happened in one year, but in 2020, they did, along with several others (Salo, 2020). Then, of course, the pièce de resistance: novel coronavirus-19 (COVID-19).

The monstrous, chaotic events of 2020 were barely behind me as I penned this book. Virtually every person on Earth was affected by global mandatory business closures, travel bans, and shortages on things as mundane as toilet paper. Some people were affected more than others in ways both seen and unseen. Depression, bankruptcy, suicide, eviction, and too many other side effects to list ran rampant, paralleling the overwhelming unpredictable effects of the illness itself.

Almost everyone knows someone who lost somebody to COVID-19, if not more than one person. Some deeply unfortunate people lost their entire family and were left desperately wondering how to go on through this unspeakable change in their lives. 2020 was a year full of events and changes no one planned for, not even the experts who were supposed to plan for any and all doomsday possibilities. The people of the world felt blindsided. The atmosphere seemed to grow heavier with the residue of anxiety, fear, anger, and sadness hanging in the air like thick humidity on a summer day in a rainforest.

Change was on everyone's mind on New Year's Eve 2020. The entire globe was anxious to usher in 2021. Hope rang in the new year louder than ever before. We had hope for a public vaccine, hope for the reopening of small businesses, hope for schools resuming, and hope to see family again, or for the first time in the case of babies born while travel bans were still in effect.

This last example is part of my own story. My sweet baby girl was born December 22, 2020. We were still living in Okinawa, Japan, because of my husband's military assignment. No family was allowed to travel to Japan. She didn't meet her family until July 2021. She was almost seven months old. Thinking about it still makes me tear up. We underwent that major life change under the cloaking shadow of isolation.

Many of us felt forced into change in 2020, but the unpredictable nature of change wasn't unique to 2020. Change can show up in your path on any day. It could be on a cool April day while you're cheering on runners at the finish line of the Boston Marathon. One minute you're standing there waiting for someone you know to go by so you can shout encouragement. The next minute you're waking up in the hospital, listening to medical staff discuss the viability of your leg! It happened just that fast the day Rebekah Gregory's world changed.

One minute Rebekah is upright with her young son sitting on her feet, then next minute, she was laid out on the sidewalk looking sideways at the chaos that had literally exploded around her. The world watched too. The scene at the finish line of the Boston Marathon in 2013 was previously unimaginable to most anyone who wasn't a military member. The letters IED (Improvised Explosive Device) weren't used as an acronym in daily conversation between members of the general public. That was a combat reality, not something that happened to an innocent bystander at a sports event.

Her book *Taking My Life Back: My Story of Faith, Determination, and Surviving the Boston Marathon Bombing* is truly inspiring. In it, Gregory reveals the ways she worked through her very unexpected and unwanted change. She made mistakes, she struggled, she broke down, but she also grew. "We certainly can't always control our lives, but we can control how we meet challenges," Gregory says.

Why now? Why is a book on change important now? For three reasons. First, we're all evolving in the wake of our own personal experiences linked to how we were affected by the events of 2020. Second, we are learning about *how* we experienced the events and *how* we learned from those changes. Third, we need to help each other make those changes stick or make other changes.

Coaching Question: How did the events of a challenging life season bring about change in your life?

WE'RE ALL EVOLVING

I joined a team of determined coaches in March 2020 on a journey to inspire people to try new things in every life arena. Our team boldly reached out to people from every walk of life and encouraged them to join the community we were building. Collectively we would push each other toward our unique goals. We called these goals and the new things people tried while pursuing them "first times and new experiences." We looked to inspire people to try rock-climbing, white-water rafting, hiking, crocheting, woodworking, yoga, cooking, grilling, and any other "new-to-them" experience you can think of. The team was fired up to get people excited and move people forward in their lives.

Then lockdowns were implemented.

The months dragged on, and our energy waned. We knew our clients were out there, but the people's adventurous spirits seemed to have been tucked away with the business suits and ties when living remotely became the new normal. We had a three-day summit planned, in-person coaching opportunities, meet up days, and small group workshops all scheduled. One by one, our summit, coaching sessions, meet ups, and small groups were canceled until the calendar was blank.

Like many other small businesses, this was not a situation we had ever foreseen. Our entire team's game plan was trashed in a matter of months because we could not provide the service model the market was used to receiving. The constraints surrounding our model had changed, and we had to evolve how our clients received and interacted with our services or we would cease to exist.

The team doubled down on its digital footprint. We offered live webinars, virtual meet ups, video call coaching sessions, videos of us having new experiences in our homes, and "around the house" scavenger hunt challenges to fire up our fans. We got really creative, tried a lot of approaches, scrapped several others, and ultimately got into a whole new rhythm as a team.

We evolved. We continued to express our team identity through our offerings to our clients. Had we not been pushed to change our approach, our team would not have grown as close as we did. We also wouldn't have learned as much as we did about our clients, their needs, the ways we could reach them, and our industry.

Personal life changes are evolving, too. Having a team to navigate that evolution with was great, but that may not be your situation. Maybe your personal change plan has had to evolve due to circumstances beyond your control, like my friend Henry and his family.

Henry had been in the US Air Force for twenty-two years. He'd finally decided to hang up his military flight suit for good and go fly for an airline when 2020 came around. His five-year plan to retire, move back to his hometown, build a house, and climb the commercial pilot ladder before he turned fifty all came to an abrupt stop. The whole family let out a collective sigh of relief that he had not yet submitted his retirement paperwork because that meant he wasn't out of a job. The only trouble was he still had a job he didn't really want.

Henry liked flying, but he wasn't doing much of it anymore. He'd worked really hard to achieve a fairly senior rank, and with that came more personnel responsibilities. His days consisted of a lot more administration work than time at the controls of his aircraft. He was burnt out and was really looking forward to retiring so he could focus on flying again. He still needed a change but had to evolve what that change looked like.

Rather than continuing down the expected path for his rank and career field, Henry decided to break from that. He took what some people would see as a backward step, but it got him more flying time. He assumed leadership of a smaller unit than what he was qualified for. He is happy with this decision. He still got the much-needed change he desired, and while it may not set him up well for a promotion, that next promotion no longer matters due to his impending retirement.

Just because a change doesn't look how you initially thought it would doesn't mean it doesn't move you toward your ultimate reality. Evolution commonly goes hand in hand with change. If you've been to college, did you graduate with the same major you started out with? Or did your plan evolve along with your needs and experiences?

Forces beyond your control will affect your plans for change. That is certainly the story for many of us in the wake of 2020. Thoughtfully evolving your plans is what will still carry you toward the vision you have for your future eighty-year-old living room.

> **Coaching Question:** *How did your initial plans for change have to evolve during the challenging season you identified in the previous question?*

WE'RE ALL LEARNING

Times of great change bring people together over the big thematic questions surrounding those changes. I had the opportunity to speak with Bill Burnett, co-author of *Designing Your Life: How to Build a Well-Lived, Joyful Life* and professor at Stanford University for over thirty years. Bill is a product designer by trade and a human enthusiast by conviction. He deeply enjoys the intersection of his trade and conviction: helping people see how they can "design" their life through the processes a product designer would leverage while creating the next big, multimillion-dollar profiting gadget (like the Apple laptops he worked on). I asked him, "What are you telling people right now, in our 2020 chaos, to inspire them to overcome their situations when they feel like they've been presented with a change they have to make that just sucks?"

Bill's response to my question captured the heart of the harness change approach. Bill said you should approach less-than-ideal changes thinking, "Alright, I'm going to see what the situation is, and given that the constraints have changed, how many options for the way forward can I brainstorm? How many different ways can I express the things I want?" What's the range of choices you have (the many possible versions of you) to get through, or to reframe, this change in your life? How do you roll with losing your job or whole industry? How do you recover after losing your home? How do you successfully move out of your parent's home, college, or first rental into something you own? What's next now that you aren't going to be a stay-at-home parent?

Part of Bill's design process is what he calls prototyping. This is the learning part of the process. It makes space for you to try things, learn from them (what works and what doesn't), and evolve your plan from those lessons learned. When faced with a change that "just sucks," Bill recommended during our interview that "Now more than ever, you need to double down on the designers' mindsets. Get curious. Collaborate, rapidly and radically, with everybody you can talk to. Try lots of stuff, prototype lots of stuff; that keeps you moving, and moving is learning.

How will you ever know you aren't cut out to be a subway train operator if you never talk to one? Bill doesn't mean that to prototype you need to spend a day in the life of every person you can think of, actually walking in their shoes. He does mean you should do some research and learn everything you can about the options you are considering. Also, examine what and how you learned from experiences you had.

In the military, after training exercises, participants are asked to submit an After Action Report (AAR), and there is what's called an After Action Meeting. This is the meeting where everyone who was involved in the training exercise comes together to discuss what they learned from the training. They talk about what went well that should be repeated in the next training exercise and what went wrong that should be fixed before the next one. It's a dedicated space for reflection and revising plans for future use. Bill suggests something similar in his designing process. I suggest you do an AAR on your most recent life change (whether it's based on 2020 events or not). Think about what you learned from that experience and begin to envision what your next prototype will look like for your next change.

Coaching Question: What did you learn from the changes you navigated during the trying season you identified?

WE CAN HELP EACH OTHER

Change, especially unforeseen change, will take an emotional toll on all of those involved. "It's so easy to get discouraged, and it's so easy to think nothing matters, particularly if you've lost a loved one or a job or career or a whole industry has disappeared from underneath you," Bill solemnly stated in our interview.

Successful change is never done alone. It takes support from those all around us to bring about lasting change. A change I walked through years ago may be a change you are currently going through. I could potentially be a great resource for you. Your neighbor could be stuck in the exact same change crisis you were stuck in at some point previously, and you could have the key to their solution. If we don't reflect on what we've learned from our changes, we won't know how to help each other.

Just like they tell you at the beginning of a flight as the crew runs through the emergency information, "First put the oxygen mask on yourself and make sure you're okay. Then you help others. If you're not taking care of yourself, you can't be in service to your own mission or to anybody," Bill said. You've got to take care of yourself throughout changes before you can successfully help anyone else.

Be a student of your own change. Examine what evolved, how you made it through, and what you learned after each change you go through, then be on the lookout for people who could benefit from your AARs. This is the honing and sharpening process. No change ever stands alone, yours or the changes of those you can help. The reflective work is how the brain rewiring becomes permanent, so your growth mindset is your automatic response. This is how you become skilled at change—by studying it to help your future self and those around you.

Now is the right time for you to be reading this book because there will always be changes to be made in all of our lives. Taking the lessons we've each learned from our own experience and the collective experiences of 2020 (or any other particularly trying year like, say, 2012 when the Twinkie was discontinued . . . and then brought back) is what is important. Evolving where necessary during change, learning from that change, and then helping others with the knowledge gained from our own experiences is what makes the skill of change an important discussion.

Coaching Question: Who in your life circle would benefit from hearing your story from that challenging season you identified in previous questions, as they are working through something similar?

PART 2

HOW TO HARNESS CHANGE

CHAPTER 4

DON'T HESITATE

———

Hesitation increases in relation to
risk in equal proportion to age.

—ERNEST HEMINGWAY

"Who ever thought an apple would change the world?" my grandfather would say every time he launched into his story about stocks he didn't buy. I hear his voice and his laugh at his own subtle joke in my head as clearly today as I did as a child sitting on an upturned five-gallon bucket in his driveway as he tinkered on some project car. I didn't understand the point of this story back then. I was somewhere between nine and eleven, so what kid would? I do now, though. He wasn't talking about an actual apple, Apple the company, or the stocks. He was talking about change.

Bob, my grandfather, was born in 1927 to a coal mining family in West Virginia. He was a kind, loyal man who believed in hard work, family, and reliability. His tranquil, routine world was rocked, like that of so many other young men, when Adolf Hitler could no longer be ignored, and the United States entered World War II. Bob served in the Navy as an electrician's mate on ships in the far-off waters of the Pacific Ocean and Philippine Sea. After the war, Bob returned to West Virginia, seeking shelter from war's turmoil in the familiarity of his home where nothing ever really changed.

Home *had* changed, though. Bob's friends had also gone off to war. Many of those friends had not returned. His middle school sweetheart had married someone else. The town now held more ghosts and heartache than welcomed consistency. Bob bore down and made a big change, hoping it would be his last. He moved to Ohio where some of his extended family lived, and he started a new, quiet life. He took a job with Thompson Ramo Wooldridge Inc. (TRW Inc.) and stayed on board for forty years. Routine was finally reestablished for Bob, but the world continued to change.

"Don't wait around like I did, Sarah Lynn," my grandfather would tell me at the end of his stock story. Apple went public in 1980, and Bob didn't buy a cent's worth of the stock. He wouldn't have bet the house on the stock's success, yet he always regretted not buying any. Not just that he didn't buy any actual stock, but that he didn't buy into the change. He resisted it to the very end. He didn't own a computer in his lifetime. He quit tinkering on cars when they became too computerized. He was late in owning a cell phone and a digital watch. Bob resisted the biggest technological changes of the second half of his life because he was fearful of them.

"I don't understand how they work or why people think they need them," he told me, referring to computers. My grandfather felt everything, cars especially, worked great just the way they were. He didn't see why having objects "think" for themselves was such a good idea. He resisted the changes brought on by technology for so long that by the time he thought he'd give some a try, he was overwhelmed and behind the learning curve.

I tried to show him how to use my Nokia 3310 cell phone. This was as basic as it got. The screen was one color, there was no internet capability, and there were only two games available to install, and it still looked like a landline phone found in most homes. He did alright with the phone part of it, but I lost him to a glazed over, mildly panicked look when I started showing him the address book and text messaging capabilities. "Do I have to text?" he asked and was relieved when I told him no.

My grandfather did eventually get a cell phone, literally the very same one I had showed him how to use. I gave it to him as a hand-me-down when I got an upgraded phone. He carried it around and made sure to keep it charged, but that was it. He'd answer it if it rang, but he never made any calls. If he did need to call someone while he was out, he would ask the first younger person he could find to help him. Bob had hesitated when change came, and change left him behind.

Big changes are intimidating, and they may cause you to hesitate, especially if you don't understand the core of them. E.M. Rogers developed the Diffusion of Innovation (DOI) Theory in 1962 as one way to explain how a product or idea gains popularity in a group or society. There are five types of adopters described by Rogers's theory. The innovators are the people driving the change. The early adopters are the people willing to take the risk on the change ahead of all others. The early majority is the group of people who see the success the early adopters have had with the change and want the same success now with less risk since the early adopters have tested it. The late majority is the group of people who are fairly risk-averse and really want to see the change was successful for the early adopters and early majority before joining in the change. Finally, the laggards are the people who do not understand what is driving the change, are very risk adverse, and only adopt the change because they cannot keep functioning in society without it (LaMorte, 2019). Apple products are both technology products and big ideas that society has largely adopted. Bob was absolutely a laggard on the DOI curve.

Treat change like an idea on the DOI curve every time. You may not be the innovator of the change. This change may be one that was forced upon you because of circumstances beyond your control, but you can own how you accept this change. Aim for the middle of the curve! Do your research, plan, and take charge. Don't get left behind and become a laggard.

> *Coaching Question: When have you hesitated in the past when change has presented itself?*

HALTED BY THE TIMELINE

I mentioned interviewing Bill Burnett in the previous chapter. At the end of that interview, Bill told me a story about someone who came to one of his Designing Your Life workshops. This woman came up to him at lunch after working unsuccessfully on her Odyssey plan. She said she was struggling to leave her high-power law position to pursue something else. She hated her job even though she was hugely successful and had made a big name for herself. She'd been thinking about making a change for a while now but just couldn't seem to get past the timeline hurdle.

Bill encouraged her several times in the course of their conversation to take the leap. The woman kept emphasizing she was already middle-aged, with a family, and very well established, so starting down a path that would potentially take years was just out of the question. "You just don't understand," she told Bill.

Bill did understand. The woman's change, should she decide to try it, would be uncomfortable and long. It would not be a movie trailer; it would be a full-length feature film. She didn't know what she wanted to do, just something that wasn't law and wouldn't take too long to switch to. There are some roles you need to get into before a certain age, the military for example, and some roles that do have an extensive training process, like becoming a neurosurgeon, which takes about twelve years (Ng, 2019). Other than those examples though, most timelines regarding jobs are not insurmountable.

More often than not, at the core of the timeline conundrum that makes people hesitate is the uncomfortable lifestyle change that comes with it. This woman had "made it." Her current lifestyle involved a large home and two Teslas. Deciding to start over in a new role would mean returning to school for potentially lengthy training *and* entry-level pay. She would be starting over at the bottom of her new career field.

She hesitated and ultimately decided not to change. She felt the discomfort that would have come from that change was too much. She'd rather live an unhappy professional life, daunted by the timeline, than be uncomfortable for a bit to get all-around life satisfaction.

Change doesn't have to happen all at once. You can take most changes in pieces. Had she acted on her desire for change sooner, the timeline wouldn't have been so long. She could have started taking the initial steps (self-reflection, researching, setting goals) before she took the big leap of leaving her position. This would have also eased the pay concern. Hesitating to do anything at all is what got her stuck in a resistance mindset next to the timeline hurdle.

> **Coaching Question:** *What has the timeline hurdle kept you from pursuing?*

THE GOLDEN PATH

The woman above had told Bill about the path she took to become the successful lawyer that she was. She went to great schools known for the quality of their law programs, clerked with renowned firms, and worked her way up in the firm she was ultimately hired by. She walked the corporate success path, or as we called it in the Navy, the golden path. It's the expected path, the path that has been walked time and time again to the point it almost seems like the only way to get to the ultimate goal. All the changes along the path are known and expected, so they are less change and more script.

Walking the same golden path as others who have gone before you is absolutely acceptable, unless it doesn't fit your situation. If the golden path causes you to hesitate and keeps you from successfully making change in your life, it's time to think beyond the path. My friend Dayana knows something about walking a unique path.

Dayana thought she wanted to be a lawyer and focus on women's rights cases in her home country of Columbia. She had a great job with a law firm, she was climbing the ladder as was expected of her, and she was looking at law school options. She was taking all the right steps along the golden path paved by many others before her, but she felt hallow. She dreamed of having a big impact in the world but didn't see this path taking her there. She knew deep down what she wanted to do, but the changes necessary to achieve it were enormous.

"I have always known I wanted to work with women and children, ever since I was a little girl. Back then, it looked like I would work as a lawyer to fight for global women's rights," Dayana told me over smoothies one day. She tried that version of her plan, and it didn't seem to fit as well as she'd hoped. From the business clothes and heels to the paperwork and lunch meetings, everything about working with the law firm ate at her. She still definitely wanted to work with women and children but had to change the "how" of her path. She determined step one would be immersing herself in a new country and learning the language. "I knew I needed to speak more languages, not only Spanish and English but even more languages, to be able to have a global impact."

At age twenty-one, she packed up and moved to the United States from Columbia to further her English capabilities.

"Going to law school in the States takes thousands and thousands of dollars I just couldn't afford right away." She changed her "how" and studied education and psychology. She changed another part of her path by taking other non-law related jobs where she could interact with women and children while also going to school. She was a live-in nanny for a little while, and then she worked with the Social Security office as a Spanish translator for the women who came there. It was here she discovered the universal language of childbirth and started setting the goals for her next big change.

To have a global impact, not only did she feel she needed to speak many languages, she also needed a field that wouldn't require recertification at every country border like law would. That realization, and her previous realization about childbirth being a universal language, led her to research doulas and midwives. "What better way to help women and children's rights than by defending the right to give birth?"

Years of harnessing change, knowing who she ultimately wanted to become, and overcoming hurdle after hurdle has gotten Dayana to where she is today. She is truly a global citizen, having an impact on the women and children she works with. She is a Colombian married to an American living in Japan. She speaks multiple languages and foresees more global opportunities to serve women and children as the military continues to move her husband around the world.

At any point along the way, Dayana could have stopped changing. She could have settled for the expected path and made the best impact she could in that corner of the world, but she persisted. The living room she pictures for herself when she's eighty is full of pictures of the places she's traveled and the mothers and babies she's helped.

When we are young, we don't have any real concept of what is "off limits" to us or that there are golden paths. We haven't been subjected to the "boxes" society tends to try to force us into. We still think we can do anything however we want to do it. If you were lucky, you had someone in your life pushing you to dream big, saying you could be anything you put your mind to. Someone encouraged you not to wait around like my grandfather did for me. He would tell anyone who would listen that his baby was going to be an architect, an engineer, an astronaut, or whatever my most recent big dream was. In his eyes, nothing was too big for me. If that meant I was going to be a veterinarian on Mars, then so be it.

The risk that comes with choosing the unique path is standing out, which often carries some notion that it is a negative, intimidating place to be. This negativity is what causes people to hesitate here. General George S. Patton is known to have said, "If everyone is thinking alike, then somebody isn't thinking." That not-thinking somebody could be you if you resist a potential change in your life because the typical path doesn't fit your situation. You could be stuck on the golden path feeling trapped.

Both the timeline hurdle and the golden path conundrum are symptoms of a bigger issue: not expecting good things or success. Maybe we hesitate when we look at the timeline because we keep thinking, "What if it doesn't work out? What if it takes longer than I thought?" Hesitating when the path to success looks like it won't work for you may have you mentally conjuring up scenes similar to the movie *Carrie*, with obnoxious high school students saying, "They're all gonna laugh at you" (De Palma, 1976). As the saying goes, "It's better to try and fail than to never have tried at all." Don't hesitate. Harness change when it comes your way, even if the path looks like an uncut field.

Coaching Question: What would the unique path look like in this change for you? Would it be a beneficial way to go rather than following the golden path?

CHAPTER 5

LIVING ROOM VALUES

——

When your values are clear to you,
making decisions becomes easier.

—ROY E. DISNEY

Buz made up his mind at the ripe old age of eight. He was going to go to the US Naval Academy, join the Navy, and be the captain of a destroyer someday. His dad had been a naval officer, as had a great uncle and several other close family friends. The stories of their careers colored Buz's memories of family gatherings. These fantastic tales of adventure about service at sea from such influential people sounded like they were pulled straight from a thrilling fiction novel, and he was captivated.

Even at such a young age, Buz understood these storytellers were instilling more in him than just history and interest in ships. These stories conveyed the values of the storytellers: integrity, service (to others and to country), tradition, respect, and hard work. It was because of these stories, and the values their tellers held, that Buz began to dream about the kind of person he wanted to become. It's the stories we have been told in our own lives that help us to imagine our ultimate destination the same way Buz did. If only we could all be as fortunate as Buz to clearly understand these lessons at the age of eight.

Buz grew up in Atlantic City, New Jersey, where he was exposed to the ocean on a daily basis. He could frequently be found looking east over the water, imagining his own adventures. His certainty grew with each passing day—his destiny lay at sea! He charted his course toward a Navy career and set his heart on one day attending and graduating from the US Naval Academy and commissioning as an Ensign (the entry-level Naval officer rank).

For the course to work, he thought he stood the best chance if he attended a "Navy" high school, so he begged his parents to send him to the Admiral Farragut Academy just one hour from Atlantic City. Farragut was modeled after the US Naval Academy and had a great college preparation curriculum, plus, he got to wear a navy-style uniform. His greatest dream was starting to come together.

Everything was on track for success by Buz's senior year. His grades were solid, he was the top-ranking cadet (a.k.a., student) at the school, and he had secured the required Congressional nomination to attend the US Naval Academy (USNA). All that was missing was the actual acceptance letter from the academy, but that acceptance letter never came. Instead, Buz was notified that while he had a great record, he had been placed on the alternates list and was informed he'd be notified if he was moved up to the acceptance list.

Buz was crushed, demoralized, and he even felt somewhat betrayed by his beloved Navy. As Buz related this story to me in our conversation, he admitted his thoughts at the time: "How could they not take me? No one could possibly want to be a Naval officer more than me! This was hands down the biggest defeat of my eighteen years." This was a change that could completely derail his plan, and it wasn't one he'd asked for, much less considered.

Dejected and despondent, Buz reached out to his "backup" school, the US Merchant Marine Academy (USMMA). He accepted their offer to join the class of 1979. He confessed to me the only reason the USMMA even made the cut as a backup was because students can commission into the Navy upon graduation. USMMA isn't as well known as the USNA, and students aren't solely trained to operate naval ships. Students of the USMMA mainly study how to operate large, commercial shipping vessels (think huge cargo ships carrying everything from dog toys to gigantic dump trucks). Buz did not see the fun, or relevancy, of this in his plan to become captain of a destroyer. His new plan was to attend the USMMA for a year and reapply to the USNA as soon as possible.

Buz arrived at the USMMA on a steamy Long Island July morning in 1975, with his heart only partially invested. He felt like he was accepting second best, and it showed on his face and in his body language. The first upper class cadet training officers who saw him recognized Buz's attitude and decided to help him become more "invested" in the process. He vividly remembered being told, "Welcome Aboard Plebe Candidate, now drop and give me twenty-five inspired push-ups!" Such encounters became a daily occurrence, and one year at the USMMA quickly began to feel like it would be an eternity.

During the second week of summer indoctrination training (after Buz had lost count of all the attitude-adjusting push-ups he'd done), his class was herded down to the waterfront marina for small boat training in power and sail craft. That's where he first saw the *Jerry Land*, a handsome forty-six-foot (14.02 m) long pilothouse trawler. Curious about this pleasure craft in a military academy marina, he jokingly asked one of the upperclassmen about who got to keep their yacht at the Academy. The other student told Buz it was actually a new boat just donated to the Academy for training the students on the intramural Power Squadron Team about the basics of power craft ship handling. Ship handling skills would be something Buz would need as a destroyer captain for sure, and he decided right then to join the Power Squadron Team.

Buz was given command of the *Jerry Land* just five months after first seeing her. Buz had been operating small power vessels for years at that point and routinely navigated vessels up to twenty feet (6.1 m) larger than the *Jerry Land*, so he was at home at her helm. Now, things were starting to get complicated where Buz's life plans were concerned, and he was forced into some serious reflection. "What was it I *really* wanted? Was it to attend the Naval Academy or to be a commissioned officer in the Navy? What was the best path to prepare me to be the best officer I could be? Was there anywhere else where I could be given command of a government vessel at this stage of my career and get the hands-on training I was getting at the USMMA?" These were all questions Buz asked himself.

Taking time to look at things objectively and being willing to recognize and accept a better path that an unanticipated change had presented led Buz to a whole new understanding of the way life could work. There wasn't *one* correct path to who he ultimately wanted to become; there were multiple. A new course to his ultimate destination began to take shape.

Forgetting about the US Naval Academy and fully committing to the US Merchant Marine Academy proved to be one of the best decisions Buz would ever make. This decision led to his very rewarding and successful thirty-four-year career in the US Navy with five commands and a service-wide reputation as a "Mariner's mariner." As for *Jerry Land*? Buz purchased her from the USMMA as a young lieutenant a few years after he graduated. He lived aboard her for over twelve years and owned her for a total of thirty one years. Now he has a hand-crafted scale model of the *Jerry Land* in his living room. This beloved piece of memorabilia conjures up countless memories of standing at her helm with his hand on her wheel, finally understanding the role she played in steering him on the right course long before he knew it was the right course! To think, it all started with the family stories, values, and dreams of who he ultimately wanted to become.

Coaching Question: Who did you dream of becoming when you were younger? Who or what do you credit with instilling your values in you? There can be more than one person, and it could even be an institution like your school.

WHAT ARE VALUES?

Buz's story is unique and insightful. His clarity of thought helped him through changes and life planning with more ease than most people. Alas, I'm not Buz. You're probably thinking the same thing: I wish I'd been as clear on my desires and values at eight-year-old as Buz was.

Buz had such a clear vision of who he was, who he wanted to be, and how he was going to get there. He took situations in stride and changed so he would remain aligned with his ultimate vision and values. We don't all have a clear picture in our eight-year-old brains of our values and how we want them reflected in our lives. In fact, if you ask most people, they will initially struggle to pinpoint *any* value they hold close, much less be able to paint a word picture of their future living room when asked the question "What does your living room look like when you are eighty?"

I like to ask that question of my coaching clients who are wrestling with change. Values are the foundations of our lives. They anchor every decision, and change, we make. However, so few people dedicate time to concretely identifying their core values beyond the belief statements in which they manifest. Values are abstract and can be difficult to define with just one word, and that's why I say they manifest in belief statements. Take, for example, the value of relationships. Common belief statements that reflect this value are "Family comes first," "It's all about community," or "The people are the best part about my job."

Christine Duvivier, a Coaching and Positive Psychology (CaPP) Institute instructor, taught me throughout my life coach training courses that "values drive motivation." It is the simplest definition of values I have heard to date. Christine expanded on that definition by saying, "Values are those things you take action to gain or keep." You know inside of you that you won't compromise your values for anything. If you've read, or heard, Simon Sinek's *Start with Why*, then you can see your values are *your* "why." They are your reason for making decisions. They are *"why"* you behave a certain way. They are also *"why"* you decide to trust or be loyal to someone, or something, or not to be.

Values initially seem abstract. Belief statements are one way of making them clearer in our minds. The exercise of visualizing them manifested in the items within your future living room is another way to give them more relatable substance. The model of the *Jerry Land* Buz keeps in his living room is an example of how abstract values can be reflected in physical items. The *Jerry Land* reminds Buz of hard work, education, and service. Those are the values he holds dear and stood by as he trained to operate first the *Jerry Land* and eventually many larger vessels.

Values aren't just for individuals. Successful organizations spend hours crafting mission statements, vision statements, and all other in-house publications to revolve around the values they chose as the foundation of their organization. These values are also often subtly visually reflected in the business logo. Organizations do this to unite their personnel around a central core of expectations.

I attended the US Merchant Marine Academy, Buz's alma mater, for my undergraduate degree. One of the first lessons we learned was the school's core values: courage, service, and teamwork. We learned these values by shouting them as loud as we could at school assemblies in the form of one big belief statement. That statement went like this: "Our values are: Courage in adversity; Service above self; and Teamwork, sir, Teamwork!" In an auditorium of over three hundred students, that has a huge and loud impact, especially on those of us who had never spent any time thinking about values. Repeating this belief statement over and over again led me to adopt these values as my own, which put words to abstract ideas I knew I had that were guiding my steps.

New York Times best-selling author of *Atomic Habits: An Easy & Proven Way to Build Good Habits & Break Bad Ones* James Clear compiled a fairly thorough list of core values that highlights authenticity, competency, justice, and trustworthiness, to name a few. Some of the values he names may resonate with you, and some may not. Clear recommends selecting no more than five, and I agree. "If everything is a core value, then nothing is really a priority" (Clear, 2018). Plus, many more than five and it becomes not only difficult to stay committed to them but also difficult to commit them all to memory. You want them to be as definitive and concise as possible so you can clearly see how they are revealed in all the decisions you make as you approach any change.

> **Coaching Question:** *What are your core values? Why are these values important to you? If you asked your closest confidant to identify one or two of your values, what would they identify?*

EIGHTY-YEAR-OLD YOU

Part of this book is me gently challenging you to look down your road in life to who you ultimately want to become: Who you want to be when you are eighty years old, or more, and how your life changes are reflected in your living room. Given that, I figured including a story from someone who has a living room and is eighty years old was a must. What treasures or knickknacks fill the room that speak to their life and the changes they endured? How has it evolved? Who are they, and how is that reflected in the items they've chosen to display? All of my grandparents passed years ago, and neither of my parents is in their eighties yet, so I had no immediate access to anyone who fit the profile. I needed help! A few emails, chats, text messages, and phone calls later, I located a classmate who felt her mother could be just what I was looking for.

Sandy is an octogenarian (she's over eighty years old). She lived through the aftermath of the Great Depression, saw World War II change our world forever, and watched as the country dove into several more wars, ended segregation, elected its first female vice president, and all the other national changes in between. She went from being the daughter of two "city slickers" (as she called them) to the daughter of hard knock farmers just trying to keep food on the table and a roof over their heads. Through it all, some foundational values grew roots in Sandy: perseverance, adaptability, and family.

Sandy was faced with an unanticipated change later in life when the state she lived in issued her a notice reclaiming her home and land for a public works project. I can count on one hand how many times I've met someone who has given up their property due to notice of eminent domain. It's not something that happens often. Sandy embraced it and saw it as a great opportunity to move back to where her husband grew up. His health was declining, and she wanted him to spend his final years surrounded by boyhood memories.

Homes in the area Sandy was shopping in were selling quickly. She kept an eye on the papers every day, and as soon as she saw something that had potential, she made the trip out to look at it. She was in love with its grounds and location the moment she set foot on the property. She wasted no time purchasing it and making plans to move well before the deadline in her eminent domain notice. Only one piece of the puzzle remained, and Sandy didn't think it would be an issue. She was wrong.

He hated it. Sandy watched her husband slowly lumber through the empty home in his childhood neighborhood the first time she showed it to him. He paused to rest several times but didn't look around or ask any questions during these breaks. He had nothing positive to say and was visibly relieved when they got back in the car to head home. By the time they got back to their house, he'd told Sandy that he refused to move, leaving her in tears. She thought the change would bring him memories of happy, lighter, childish times as his health continued to fade. She thought he'd like the change in scenery and the ease of access to his doctors compared to their current commute. She thought he'd appreciate being back in the energizing hustle and bustle of the city.

Unfortunately, she had assumed incorrectly. Now she was stuck with a home her husband refused to move into and was on the verge of losing her current home. Sandy was at a loss and frozen. She chose to wait for someone or something to make the decision for her. That something came four years later with the passing of her husband. She was now free to move to the home she'd purchased, just in time to comply with the deadline of the eminent domain requirement. She was looking forward to the fresh start, proximity to family, ease of access to all the things a big city can offer, and the garden grounds she'd fallen in love with on her first visit. Having learned to plant, cultivate, and harvest all sorts of fauna during the hard times after the Depression, Sandy had always kept a garden to keep her rooted in her identity as a survivor.

The garden space of her new home was one of the key selling points for her. When the movers came to pack up and move her downtown, she asked them to pack up the stones from her current garden's retaining wall. They held great meaning and memories for her. One day, back on the family farm, her husband had seen a truck going down their road with a full load of beautiful, dark gray and forest-brown stones. The driver caught a flat tire, and her husband went out to help. As a thank-you, the driver gave her husband some of the stones. Sandy had learned a bit of masonry while growing up on her family farm and used those stones in her marriage home to tie her new life to her childhood farm. Now, living downtown, she can see those stones in the wall she built around her new garden from her living room every day. They are an hourly reminder of who she is, where she came from, what matters most, and all the changes she's made throughout her long life that led to this beautiful view.

Coaching Question: What's in your living room when you're eighty? What does each of those items say about your life? How do those items reflect your values?

GLASSES AND MEMORABILIA

Looking at your values with your changes (past, present, and yet to come) in mind will frame those changes in a new light. This perspective will help solidify your drive and resolve for making all change. Changes made with your values in mind will feel even more personal than they already do because they are bonded to the core of who you are.

Values are like the lenses of glasses. When you have the wrong prescription in your glasses, you aren't going to see clearly. If the doctor got your prescription wrong or the lenses weren't crafted properly, you might as well not wear glasses at all. It's when the prescription is correct, the lenses are ground accurately, and the glasses sit properly on your face that you can see perfectly. Looking at life through the wrong "lenses," the wrong values (or even no values at all), means you aren't going to see your life, your hopes, or your dreams clearly.

Memorabilia are those things we keep that tell the stories of our lives, the dreams we imagined, the goals we achieved, and the memories we made. When I ask my coaching clients to picture themselves in their living rooms at age eighty, I ask them what memorabilia is present. It can be a 5K race medal, a picture of some exotic place, a book signed by someone who inspired them, or a great many other things they will look at and say, "This one time, I . . ." It is in these items that your values are reflected over time. These are the items you choose to keep close to remind you of how you stayed true to you through all of your life changes and endeavors.

Our values come from many different influences in our lives. The people we grew up with in our lives, our family culture, our nation's culture, the friends we make, the pop-culture figures we hold up as idols, and many more influence these values. Understanding where you gained your values from will help you better understand why you make the decisions you make and who you will ultimately become.

As you identify your core values and how they are being reflected in the items in your living room, also think about where and from whom you gained those values. Sometimes values will shift over time as our influences change, much like your eyesight changes so you may need a new prescription. Values you have now may not be what a younger you had and may not be what an older you will have. Identifying the baseline for the here and now and projecting it out will bring clarity to your current change.

I certainly had no clue who I wanted to become when I was eight years old but, after hearing Buz's story, I began to see that subconsciously, all the changes in my life have been made with my values in mind: adventure, learning, and relationship. Aha! What if I'd *consciously* thought about them at each change? What if you did too? My perspective on change shifted with this realization: If you approach any life change with the thought of "Who do I want to become?" all the pieces will come into focus and any major change will be less intimidating. You'll also be less likely to get stuck, quit, or proceed haphazardly if you focus on who you will be years from now—eighty-year-old you.

Coaching Question: How does the change you're making move you forward toward these memorabilia items, toward the eighty-year-old you?

CHAPTER 6

SET GOALS

—

If you aim at nothing, you will hit it every time.

—ZIG ZIGLAR

One of my favorite songs is "Wake Me Up" by Avicii. His voice is so rich, the rhythm of the song is perfect to run along to, and the lyrics are so relatable. He describes following his heart through dark times and hoping to travel the world, but he hasn't made any plans. He just hopes to awaken one day wiser and older.

Think about that in the context of approaching a change in your life. You're guided by your instinctive need for change. It's a little scary, and you didn't, or felt you couldn't, plan for this change so you're living on hope. You hope an opportunity comes your way. You hope it works out how you want it to. You hope you get the job, the invite, or the winning lottery numbers that will finally change your life.

Hope alone is not a life plan that most of us can live by. A professor of mine once said "Humans hate uncertainty." That is what hope is: uncertainty dressed in a pretty ball gown to make it seem like an attractive, acceptable plan. Don't get me wrong. You've got to have a healthy dose of hope whenever you decide to make any change in your life, but hope cannot be Plan A. Plan A has to be SMART.

SMART is an acronym that stands for Specific, Measurable, Achievable, Realistic, and Timely/Time-Bound. This is a method of setting goals that is commonly referenced because it is a structured, deliberate approach to mapping out success. The SMART acronym was developed by George Doran, Arthur Miller, and James Cunningham in their 1981 American Medical Association Forum article called "There's a S.M.A.R.T. way to write management goals and objectives."

This is the goal setting method I use and I urge my clients to use. This method can be applied to big goals, small goals, abstract goals, very numerically defined goals, and every goal in between. Let me show you how to be SMART about your goals through unpacking each of the letters in the acronym.

> *Coaching Question: What are the top three goals you're working toward right now? Are they SMART? How do they move you closer to who you ultimately want to become?*

GET SPECIFIC

There is a bowl of Mardi Gras beads on my living room bookcase. I was sixteen when I chose to leave my quiet Florida town and move to New Orleans with my dad. The miles of beautiful, soft, sandy beaches of my cozy Florida hometown had instilled wisdom in me that I would take with me to this new, bold destination. I learned the ocean is never the same blue from one day to the next. Watches are not necessary to go through daily life so long as you aren't afraid to ask for help. Good people stick around—in their job, their community roles, and in their families. I also learned I needed way more speed, excitement, and adventure than my tourist-dependent, no-Starbucks, two-stoplight island town could ever have to offer. So off we went to chase the neon excitement that New Orleans is famous for.

I didn't drive for the first three months I was there! (Remember what I said about two stoplights? I wasn't kidding.) I didn't have to drive since we moved only a quarter of a mile (402 m) away from my high school, which also happened to be my dad's office since he was the school's new athletic director. As time passed, we began spending more time driving around and exploring the city. To be honest, we were running out of restaurants within walking distance. We made it a point to get to a different part of the city for a new restaurant once a week. I saw all the beauty, wonder, poverty, and corruption such a diverse and historic city could offer in the three short years I lived there, and almost all of it was seen in the pursuit of food.

With every move the military has brought to my life, especially when I moved to Okinawa, Japan, with my husband in 2018, I've unpacked that bowl of beads and I have reflected on how I handled the lessons the move to New Orleans taught me. Okinawa is not a jazz capital by any means, but two things were immediately similar: First, no way would I be comfortable driving right away since they drive on the opposite side of the road from the United States and they drive *much slower*. Second, the food would be an adventure. Our 2018 move to Okinawa was not my first time experiencing the island, and I knew it wasn't my favorite place (more on that to come in the chapter on habits), so I was going to have to find a way to enjoy it.

I needed goals, but not job-related goals or competitive in anyway. I needed *life* goals, goals like: make friends, get out of the house once a day, go to more places than just our military base. These may not sound like what you think of as "goals," and that is a common misconception. We tend to think of goals as somehow only job related, habit altering (i.e., losing weight or eating better), or sports centered. Goals are anything you feel you need to accomplish. They can sometimes be difficult to define, especially when we don't initially consider them goals.

Doran, Miller, and Cunningham didn't just choose Specific as the starting point to make the acronym spell out a word. They chose it because being specific about a goal is the glue that keeps the whole structure together and moving forward, especially when it's a goal for change. Without first identifying the specifics of any change and its associated goals, none of the rest of the process can come together.

I set three specific goals to help me make the most of my time in Okinawa. First, get involved in a spouse-run volunteer organization so I could make lasting friendships. Second, start a food blog and explore the eclectic food scene on the island. Third, get involved with a local running group so I could see new places on the island while running, make some more friends, and burn a few of the calories gained from my second goal. Phrasing those goals the way I did made them way more specific than how they started out: make friends, get out of the house, go places other than base.

Envision the goal(s) of a change you want to make in granular detail: colors, smells, emotions, textures. You are the artist of your change. Your canvas is blank, and you have every color at your disposal. Or you've got a thirty-pound (13.6 kg) block of clay waiting for you to give it form. Art isn't your lingo? How about sports? Imagine you are a marathon runner lined up at the starting line 26.2 miles (42.16 km) away from the finish line. That's a long way! It can feel insurmountable thinking about it purely as a distance. If you picture crossing that finish line in specific detail—the exhausted, sweaty smile on your face as the photographers snap pictures of you turning off your watch and grabbing your medal on your way to the highly anticipated free banana—the goal begins to feel achievable.

Coaching Question: What specifics can you add to the three goals you identified to make them SMARTer?

HOW TO MEASURE AND ACHIEVE THE ABSTRACT

Measurable and Achievable are the M and A of the SMART acronym. Without setting up a way to measure your progress toward your goal, you won't know when, or if, you achieve it. Goals without ways of measuring them are wishes. Wishes, like hope, are not a Plan A for life.

Some measurements are obvious: make one hundred more products than last year, earn 0.5 more GPA points this semester than last semester, or earn the gold level of recognition points toward your volunteer award. Those are all fairly numerical and well defined. However, when we are talking about goals that go with personal change, they are usually a bit more abstract. "Be *better* at, or have *more* of, (insert goal here)" is common phrasing of personal change goals. This phrasing is too vague. How the heck do you measure *better* or *more*? Phrases like these commonly lead to people getting stuck or intimidated by their change, but not my friend Dan.

Dan worked as a diesel engineer on large cargo ships. He was routinely out on the ship for four months at a stretch and then home for four months. He made great money, so his family of four people and two dogs lived in a nice, new subdivision in a house they were close to paying off after only owning for a few years. Outwardly, he was doing great, but inwardly, he was struggling. He needed a change so he could have *more* time with his family and be a *better* dad and husband. Dan took the leap, left his stable job with the shipping union, and went to work for a shore-based, ship-related company working a traditional nine-to-five job close to their house.

On paper, Dan had more time to be at home to be a better dad and husband, but things at home didn't change the way he had expected with this extra time. He still didn't seem to be home as often as he'd thought he would be and he still didn't seem to be any better at the dad thing. When I asked Dan how he was measuring *better* and *more*, he said, "Ummm, I'm not sure."

Through some exploratory questions and reflection on his part, we put a number to *more* and some parameters to *better* that fit his vision. His measurements were doing homework with the kids two nights a week, dropping them off and picking them up three days a week, fitting in a date night each week, and cooking two nights a week to give his wife a break.

Coaching Question: How will you, or can you, measure your progress toward the goal(s) you've set?

REALISTIC AND TIMEBOUND

Dan and I also discussed how realistic these goals were. Sure, his new shore-based job did allow him to not have to leave home for work for four months at a time, but did it really allow him that much time at home with his family? Dan thoroughly examined his typical work schedule, his holiday schedule, and any future projects he had that he could reasonably project. He determined yes, those goals and measurements were realistic.

This determination took time. Dan didn't just jump in and say, "Yep, totally doable," without digging into his real situation. That is what Doran, Miller, and Cunningham mean for you to do when setting SMART goals. They intend for you to think critically about how likely it is you are truly capable of achieving the goal you want to set. For example, me as the starting center on the University of Wyoming's women's basketball team would have been a completely unrealistic goal. (Remember, I'm just tapping the measuring stick at five feet four inches (1.62 m) tall.) However, me being the starting point guard could have been realistic, albeit a stretch.

Dan and I also set a timeline of four months for his goals to become routine so he could complete the SMART acronym.

All goals need timelines so they don't drag on or become forgotten. Abstract goals, like what Dan was dealing with in trying to measure *better* dad and *more* time, especially need timelines. These goals are muddy to begin with, but with no time driving their achievement, they quickly revert to their murky ways, never to be clearly accomplished.

The more we communicate our goals and plans to others, the more likely they are to come to fruition. If other people hear you talk about your plans, they will ask about them. Dan didn't just talk to me about his goals and measurements; he got his whole family involved with keeping him accountable. Because of these conversations, his children kept track of how many times he engaged with them during the week and how many times he'd cooked dinner. On the day of his deadline, with his new routines securely in place, the whole family celebrated to solidify the achievement.

Celebrations are so important! Celebrations are the mile markers of change. They are the exclamation point at the end of the SMART acronym in my mind. Without a celebration marking a successful change, it loses some of its impact. "Your celebration does not have to be something you say out loud or even physically express. The only rule is that it has to be something said or done—internally or externally—that makes you feel good and creates a feeling of success. It could be a 'Yes!'; a fist pump; a big smile; a V with your arms. You might imagine the roar of the crowd; think to yourself 'Good job' or 'I got this'; or picture fireworks." I think B.J. Fogg was really onto something here in his article for Ideas.Ted.Com (Fogg, 2020).

Coaching Questions:

—*How will you celebrate accomplishing your SMART! goals?*

—*Who have you told, and who will you tell, about this change and its goals?*

MONOLOGUE AND DOUBTS

B.J. Fogg is a professor at Stanford University and the author of *Tiny Habits: The Small Changes that Change Everything.* His work is about changes in behavior and habits, but it can absolutely be applied to change as a whole. He often mentions motivational statements he feels you need to be saying to yourself to successfully achieve the change you are implementing in your life. Of all the people you tell about your change, you will internally talk to you about the change the most.

The tone of your internal monologue is critically important when making changes. If you internally chatter about your goals, you'll keep the plan in sight. We act when we feel supported and heard. You are the first person you told about your idea for this change. You will also be the last person you hear at night. *Your* voice has to be the most excited supporter of all the voices in your life for this to be a success. If your inner voice isn't shouting about your plans like an enthusiastic peanut salesman in a baseball stadium, then no one else will be excited about it either.

Talking with others about your goals, hopes, and dreams may not come as naturally for you as it does for others. Talking to people in general may not come very naturally for you for that matter. The benefits of talking to others regarding your change will far outweigh the scary and uncomfortable moments! People naturally want to help others, and no successful change is made alone in silence because it will go unsupported. Challenge yourself to get out of your comfort zone on this. Start with those people closest to you and work your way up to telling the coffee shop barista. Voice your desires to your universe and see what happens. I'm betting on great things.

Doubts will enter the conversation from both inside and outside. I'm not saying don't hear the doubts or ignore them. Give the doubts their airtime and see if they are founded on concrete reason or manifested in fear. Identifying your inner voice, and its tone, will go a long way in helping you identify the tone and intentions of the external voices you'll encounter.

Monologue, dialogue, and doubts add clarity to all aspects of SMART goals. Other people may be able to see other specifics you should include, see other ways to measure, help you adjust the timeline, or provide any number of other helpful insights. To tap into these insights, you've got to get out of your own head and out of your own way so you can take an active role in achieving your goals.

Coaching Question: What is the tone of our inner monologue? How can you amplify its supportive stance? For example, you could use your inner monologue to remind yourself each day of all the little wins you have had toward accomplishing the goal or you could use it to repeat the positive statements of others who you've told about your change.

CHAPTER 7

TAKE AN ACTIVE ROLE

Action is the foundational key for all success.

—PABLO PICASSO

"I cannot want your change for you more than *you* want it for yourself," I told Darlene during one of our coaching sessions. Darlene had been seeing me for over three months at that point. She had yet to make any measurable progress toward switching careers despite saying it was what she really wanted. Darlene appeared to be stuck and a little afraid to change. As soon as the words were out of my mouth, I realized I'd repeated that exact same sentence to at least three other clients just that week.

I took a moment to analyze the other similarities between Darlene and the other three. They were all seeking other employment options. They had all told me how unhappy they were with their current positions. They also all felt disconnected from themselves in their current roles and didn't feel like they got any joy out of their days.

"Darlene, what is attracting you to the new roles you've been researching?" I asked.

"Oh, well they all pay better and have more flexible hours, and their offices are closer to my home," was her very logical, unemotional response. While all of those things are great, none of them really bonds us to change. That lack of bond is why Darlene was stuck.

Darlene was an architect, so I asked her to think of her potential new career as a house under construction. I helped her to realize she was constructing her "home" before picking the site. She was looking at the sturdy walls of her potential new careers (all the logical reasons she had listed previously), but she was neglecting to inspect the plot of land. She wasn't examining what really connected any of the new careers to who she was. She didn't know what she valued in work beyond the tangibles, so she had no idea how to choose and was thus choosing *not* to change.

She wasn't alone! It was the same story with the other three clients. All four of them knew they weren't happy with their current situation, but beyond dollars and office location, they didn't understand what drew them toward other roles. This had all four of them stuck and not moving ahead with the changes they claimed they wanted to make.

I went on to ask Darlene several thought-provoking questions, including: What part of her day at work brought her joy? What work was she doing when others complemented her for her work? If I were to interview one of her coworkers, what personality traits would they say Darlene possessed? Each question was meant to have her search for how her values were reflected in the aspects of her work she enjoyed.

Then I asked her to consider how, or where, she could find roles in which she would work from her values every day. Through these questions, Darlene saw the roles she had been researching were too similar to the one she was currently in and not enjoying. None of them spoke to her peak-performance self, and none of them reflected any of her values. She realized subconsciously she knew she would be as unfulfilled in those roles as her current one. This subconscious knowledge is why she appeared to not want to change as much as I wanted her to change.

Peak performance is akin to what athletes call flow. I was on the rowing team at the US Merchant Marine Academy. The boats are long and skinny with two to eight rowing athletes seated single file in a line facing the opposite direction from where the boat is heading. Each athlete has at least one very long oar they use to propel the boat forward. The longest boat is the eight-person boat, and it can become an unstable, gangly mess very quickly if the team is not careful.

In the early stages of training, when the athletes do not know each other's style well, that is exactly what happens. No one is in sync, water is flying everywhere, the boat seems to be going nowhere, much less in a straight line, and you consider practices successful if the team makes it to the dock with no one dumped overboard along the way! Once the team has come together, though, the ride is a totally different story. The athletes have developed their physical skills and their knowledge of each other, so the boat glides through the water like a hot knife through butter. It is a magical, smooth feeling that makes all the uncoordinated learning worth the initial struggles. It is flow. This state of in-sync operation makes even the most difficult races and practices seem relaxed and natural. This state is what keeps the athletes coming back for more.

Peak performance exists in the workplace, home, and other arenas too. It's that space and task where your skills, knowledge, capability, values, and joy all intersect. Think about a time when you were doing something and you felt like you blinked and an hour had passed. You didn't notice this passing of time because you were joyfully immersed in your task. For me, my peak-performance self comes out when I'm coaching a client through any life challenge. For someone else, it could be serving meals at a local shelter. For Darlene, her peak-performance self is at the pool's edge coaching young people.

Darlene was finally able to change once she identified what had her stuck. Today, Darlene is fulfilled in her new role as a swim coach. She lives from her values every day as she helps children learn in a setting that brings her peace. She is also her own biggest champion. While she worked with me, I was a supporter for her. I encouraged her to explore options, identify her values, and figure out what role best fits her skill sets and what allowed her to work in peak performance most often. But I could not do the work for her, and neither could any of her other supporters. Ultimately, Darlene had to put in the work to make the mindful, successful change she knew she needed.

Robert Hicks, PhD, writes a monthly *Coach's Corner* in American Association of Physician Leadership's *Physician Leadership Journal*. In the May/June issue of 2020, his article was titled "Dealing with Rebellious Resistance," and in it he voices exactly what I was trying to say to Darlene: "Recognition that change is needed must come from within, not from outside pressure. In other words, for change efforts to endure, they must be driven by intrinsic motivation." No one can want your change more than you because it's your unique intrinsic (internal) motivation that will drive you into action to make the change last.

Your values are part of your intrinsic motivation. You're not going to be internally driven to do something that doesn't align with your values. I could never be a swim coach like Darlene. While we both value peace, what connects her with that value is very different from what connects me to it. Swimming is not my peaceful place. If I were trying to make a change to a role that involved a lot of swimming, I would get stuck not taking an active role in my own change.

> **Coaching Question:** *Who are you when you are in your peak performance role? What does that person value and how are those values reflected in that role?*

THINK BIG AND GO FOR IT!

Open up an internet browser, go to a search engine, and type in, "What does it mean to think big." One of the first responses will be the definition from *American Heritage Dictionary of Idioms*: "Be Ambitious." The hits following this one are similar.

Thinking big is all about being ambitious, not settling, and pushing yourself to your full potential. People who think big are people who aren't constantly adrift in life. These ambitious people have aim points for their lives and take deliberate action to arrive at those milestones. Every successful, aspiring person has intentionally planned their success from the moment they defined their vision to the moment it came to fruition. All of them used processes and skills similar to the ones in this book, whether they were conscious of it or not.

That's the difference between thinking big and dreaming. Big ambitions don't just become reality on their own; they take planning. This may sound exhausting or stressful or like it takes the joy out of the journey but keep it all in perspective. Aspirations are relative. What I aspire to is probably different from what you aspire to, and both of our aspirations will most likely be *vastly* different from SpaceX's Elon Musk. If you're looking at a change with someone else's ambitions in mind, then yes, the road to achievement will be exhausting and stressful because it won't be true to you.

You've got to think of *your* idea of big, not anyone else's idea of big. We all define big differently. It's the thinking and planning parts that will be similar.

When you were in elementary school, you were probably asked at some point what you wanted to be when you grew up. Most of us answered that question based on what we saw our role models doing or what our role models conditioned us to aspire to. I wanted to be an engineer for a long time because that is what my grandfather thought my "tinker with everything" tendencies would be best suited for. My grandfather was a huge influence in my life, and I enjoyed spending time with him, so I figured I would enjoy doing what he envisioned for me. I never did become an engineer though, just as the majority of us never become what we dreamed of in childhood. We find our own ambitions along the way. We find those paths because eventually we stop asking "what" and start asking "who."

Adam Grant is a world-renowned psychologist, professor at the Wharton School, and five-time *New York Times* best-selling author. Grant says he's "all for encouraging youngsters to aim high and dream big. But take it from someone who studies work for a living: those aspirations should be bigger than work. Asking kids what they want to be leads them to claim a career identity they might never want to earn. Instead, invite them to think about what kind of person they want to be" (Grant, 2019).

Darlene had been living the big dreams others had envisioned for her in her role as an architect. Her father had been one, and he enjoyed it, so when she was asked what she wanted to be when she grew up, she said architect. I relayed Grant's thought about "who" not "what" to Darlene, and the pieces fell into place for her. She then actively sought *her* big role that felt like who she wanted to be, rather than what she'd been conditioned to think she *should* want to be.

As you move through your life changes, dreaming *your* big dream, thinking about "who" instead of "what," be sure you are listening for *you*. Don't listen for role models, celebrities, social pressures, or any other outside influence. Tune all of that out and focus on thinking big for you and who you want to be. Then go for it! Take the necessary steps to harness your change opportunity and make it happen.

Coaching Question: Who do you ultimately want to become? What version of you is sitting in your living room when you are eighty surrounded by all of your life's memorabilia? What big-to-you ambitions are reflected there?

"JUST NOT THIS" ISN'T ENOUGH

Jerry worked in the public school system for forty two years. He coached just about every sport with a ball, and he taught middle school to high school students everything from geography to philosophy (except math—definitely not his strong suit). He thrived on teaching and coaching the next generation of lawyers, engineers, dentists, astronauts, and every other profession young people can aspire to. Then one day he got punched in the face, and that love abruptly stopped.

A fight had broken out in the bus pick-up line at the high school where Jerry worked. The two young men involved were seniors, each over six feet (1.82 m) tall and athletes of solid muscle. Jerry didn't know what the fight was about, but he knew it needed to end before any students got hurt. He stepped in between the two shouting teens and tried to deescalate the argument. Neither teen registered Jerry's arrival as punches began to fly. Jerry wasn't quite quick enough to block the right jab from one of the teens that was intended for the other angry student. Luckily, since Jerry was a bit shorter than the two teens, it wasn't a well-aimed punch. He walked away with a black eye and two suspended teens.

"I'm sixty two years old. I don't need to be catching punches from teenage drama anymore," he told me the day he decided to retire. I couldn't blame him. While fights were rare, other drama was not, and it was beginning to take its toll. Jerry looked forward to going to work every day less and less and more and more forward to his weekend round of golf. Several of his close friends were beginning to retire, and he thought their daily schedules were looking much more attractive than his.

Three days after the fight, still sporting the shiner, Jerry submitted his two weeks' notice. The opportunity for change had arrived, and he harnessed it—or so he thought. He harnessed the opportunity to *not* do what he was doing, but that was where the planning stopped. He dove headfirst into a blissfully free schedule. Waking up late, golfing as many days as his back could stand, road trips to see his children, and binge watching every movie he was even remotely interested in quickly filled the white space on his calendar. However, three years into this free-schedule existence, Jerry was over it and ready to make another change.

"Because I had nothing to aim for, I was going nowhere but toward the ultimate end, and that began to scare me," he confided in me during our interview. He had stopped actively seeking change, and the sameness was becoming unbearable. He looked around his living room at all the life reflected in its contents and started to plan for some changes.

Jerry got stuck in sameness because he didn't actively participate in shaping his change. He knew he didn't want what he had, so he dropped it. That's not the same as change. It's not quitting, either. It's the mental mud in the middle: stagnation. As we talked about in Chapter 2, the brain thrives on growth.

The neuroplasticity of change creates keeps us all evolving, seeking happiness in new ways, and owning the joy that comes from those changes. There's no joy in mental stagnation, just atrophy, which is what Jerry described.

Jerry thought back to what he truly enjoyed about his time as an educator. It was his interactions with his basketball team that kept him going back year after year. He loved watching the young boys grow and develop into mature men who had ambitions and goals of their own. He enjoyed inspiring them and gently challenging them when they seemed to get stuck. This was what he did at peak performance, when his "who" intersected his "what." This was when he was living through his values.

After some encouragement from his network and several calls to different schools, Jerry found a job coaching middle school boys' basketball again. He was back in his element. "It was the easiest change I'd made in years," he told me. "I felt again like I was who I was meant to be."

I mentioned in the introduction there are thirty one definitions for "change" in the dictionary (*Merriam-Webster,* 2021). Half of those definitions are verbs! They define action. You've got to want your change more than anyone else, and you've got to go after it from the right frame of mind. Wanting something that "just is not" your current situation won't ground you or get your inner monologue peanut-seller excited. Look at opportunities for change like the action-packed, personally imagined movies they should be and boldly think big. If you do find yourself stuck in any sort of mental stagnation, check in with your network to see what they may have to say to help you out of it.

Coaching Question: *Have you ever faced a "just not this" moment? Did you do the reflective work to make sure the change you made kept you true to your values and who you ultimately wanted to become?*

CHAPTER 8

NETWORK

———

Love, friendship, networking—these are all critical connections and the foundation of a healthy, happy life.

—WHITNEY WOLFE HERD

I'll be honest. I used to think "networking events" sounded like places where people went to try to suck up and impress other people in the hopes the new person would be able to do something for their career. It kind of felt like speed dating but without dinner and wine. The thought of handing out business cards to complete strangers both repulsed and intimidated me. Then one day, a mentor of mine changed my outlook. She told me, "Don't go into it expecting to make the quick, self-serving connection. Go into it hopeful to find a genuine, lasting, reciprocating connection."

That brought it home for me, and I expanded my definition of networking. I began to see the term "networking event" no longer just applied to a formal event hall with vendors and job hopefuls circulating each table, picking up free swag and handing out résumés. Networking events became office events with colleagues from other departments I had yet to meet, work socials with families and/or clients, trips to museums or hobby courses where I may meet similarly interested people, or, truthfully, happy hour at one of my favorite restaurants where I might meet neighbors from other apartment buildings. Networking became an everyday event.

Networking is "the activity of meeting people who might be useful to know" according to the *Cambridge Dictionary*. It is connecting with other people in a genuine, meaningful way over a shared interest or goal. It does not have to involve business cards or the corporate world at all. Networking could involve a farmer's market where you befriend the local bee farmer and make plans to visit his hives. It could involve your local library where you join a leadership book club and find a group of people who encourage you to get more involved in your local community.

You are networking whenever you are meeting people, therefore every person you have met is part of your network. Bonus points if you have remained in contact with these people in some way because those are the people you will draw from as you harness your change. Your network is your greatest resource!

It isn't just about staying in touch, though. It's about how you stay in touch and how often. What mediums are you using to *actively* connect with key players in your network? How often are you reaching them? Being active in staying connected to those in your network is so important. It's not enough to have people as just a connection on LinkedIn or Facebook. You have to keep that relationship going. As you examine your network, make note of which connections you need to reestablish. Set dates, times, and locations for these re-connections. Treat them the same way you treat goal setting. Making them SMART (remember the acronym from chapter six? Specific, Measurable, Achievable, Realistic, and Time-Bound) will ensure you do actually reconnect.

A common misconception about networking is it's cheating, asking for favors, or somehow disingenuous. Quiet that voice, if it is in your mind, because it is not right. If that voice is in your head telling you networking is like haggling with your neighbor at a yard sale over the price of some vintage Tupperware, then odds are that voice comes from an experience where someone "networked" with you and used you. Networking done right is creating authentic connections that are mutually beneficial.

Is there someone in your network that has recently done something you need or want to do, like writing a résumé for instance? Say you asked them for help, and they were more than willing to assist. They may now ask you to spread the word to others who may need their services, or they may be happy just to help and then want to know how the résumé was received. That is a mutually beneficial networking connection. You reached out for help, you received that help, and the helping party also benefited.

You might not believe me when I say this, but there are people who are happy to help and ask for nothing to return. Really! I have a friend who practically lives for it. He gets so much joy from connecting people in his network who can benefit from knowing each other that he hosts monthly dinner parties dedicated to it. Few things make him happier than hearing how one of his connections furthered the life journey of the other parties involved.

> **Coaching Question:** How are you hoping the people in your network can help you? (Make another connection for you, show you around your new neighborhood, point you in the direction of a realtor, mentorship, someone to watch your pets, etc.) In what way can you give back to the connections in your network who help you make this change so that this is an authentic, mutually beneficial connection?

THOSE CLOSEST TO YOU

Travis didn't have a vision for his living room for a long time. He didn't think he'd ever settle down. He wanted to be a military pilot, travel the world, and live life in the "fast lane" that is glorified by several songs and movies. Travis is one of my college friends. Our alma mater allowed him to begin leading the action movie life even before graduation. By the time Travis was twenty and still in college, he was sailing around the world on huge cargo ships. He pulled into shipping ports in foreign countries he'd only ever heard about on the news or in history class, which expanded his world view with each passing wave.

School was tough. The curriculum included three long years of rigorous ship training on top of regular college courses.

Graduates receive not only a college undergraduate degree but they also earn a US Coast Guard license in either ship handling or ship engineering because of the extra training. Navy pilot training, after all of that, seemed daunting to Travis. In his final year at the US Merchant Marine Academy, he decided not to pursue the pilot life. Ships were plenty capable of taking him around the world, and the lifestyle fit his never-going-to-settle-down plan. So, lacking any other concrete plan or inspiration, Travis shifted his aim from the skies to the seas.

Even the most wandering of souls long for relationship and connection. After a few difficult sailing years, Travis began to rethink his tumbleweed lifestyle. He started looking for a place to set down roots near friends. He was looking to make a change.

Corpus Christi, Texas, may not seem like the most likely of locations for a farm-raised Illinois man, but it called to him like a beacon in the fog. He had friends who lived in the city, and the nearby port was perfect to ship from. Everything he owned fit into the bed of his truck with room to spare. He packed it all up and road tripped down through the flyover states, thrilled to start this new chapter in coastal south Texas. It was enough for a while, but something was still missing.

Her name was Kim. Travis met her through his friends—his network. "She was enough for me to find a shore-based job," Travis told me as he remembered the day his world shifted. "People don't always realize how one decision changes the trajectory of your life or how your dream or desire today will change and morph into something more fulfilling later."

One change led to the most fulfilling change of Travis's life, but he didn't make it lightly or quickly.

The decision to stop sailing on his beloved cargo ships and come ashore was an adjustment of massive proportions for Travis. Kim had reservations as well since the sea was such a huge part of the Travis she had fallen in love with. However, the idea of Travis continuing to sail for most of the year on ships did not appeal to Kim's dreams of a family-centered, traditional nine-to-five life. They talked it out over a few months, being careful not to rush the important conversations and decisions. They included everyone in their network in the conversation too, so they left no stone unturned when weighing the pros and cons. Travis sailed less and less and felt happier than he ever had before. One year after meeting Kim, Travis had a shore-based job.

Then Travis proposed! They had a beautiful wedding, made a few moves for their jobs, had two kids, and bought a project car. Today they are still together and going strong. They continue to run all the major, life-changing decisions by each other and other members of their network, thoroughly making sure they are giving each change its due. Looking back on the big change of finding a shore-based job, Travis says, "The decision has allowed me to pursue a master's degree, be a homeowner, manage my debt, and plan for long-term events (vacations, new vehicles, etc.)." It has also allowed him to continue to travel, which is what he loved so much about sailing.

In Travis's living room, there is a hand-blown glass sailboat. He bought it while he and Kim were honeymooning in Italy.

It captures his life desires and his big life change perfectly and serves as a daily reminder to stay his course.

Travis and Kim's story is a success story. Not only did Travis recognize his need for change but he also recognized the need to be mindful of those closest to him in his network who would be affected by that change. He didn't rush it and was sure to have the tough conversations with Kim before making any final decisions. Your changes also won't take place in a vacuum. You'll need support from others in your network who will be affected, and they will need your support as well.

More often than not, life changes involve more people than just you. Your significant other, children, parents, extended family, and close friends will all be affected, in some way, by your decision to make change. You will set yourself up for success by having in-depth conversations with people in your life in the early planning phases of change. These relationships may be decades old, and you may feel you know how the other person will respond but *ask anyway*! The other person may respond in a way you never expected, like Sandy from Chapter 5 whose husband refused to move. The more likely situation is they will respond exactly how you expect but they will greatly appreciate that you asked. They'll be even more committed to supporting you in the change because they will feel valued and respected by you asking.

Also, talk with these key players about the short-range and long-term goals you're working toward. Talk about the "why now." Talk about how you see the change you are planning affecting them and how you plan to mitigate those effects. Ask for their input! A big bonus of these conversations when you ask for their feedback is these key players in our lives often see things we bring to the table that we don't see in ourselves. They may also see other effects we hadn't thought about. By asking for the input of your family members and network at large, you are giving them a voice and you will most likely get a lot more support from them then you would have otherwise. When it comes down to it, people just want to be heard and have a voice in what happens in their lives.

> *Coaching Question: Who, besides you, will be affected the most by this change? What support do you need from the key players in your life during this change? What support do they need from you?*

WE ALL NEED A SIMON

I heard a speaker at the spring 2021 session of the Okinawa Leadership Seminar describe three specific types of people we need in our lives. You need a person who will gently give you their opinion but won't push it too hard, a person who lifts you up no matter what, and a person who will tell you like it is even if you really don't want to hear it. The speaker, Vinny Toth, said, "We all need a Randy, Paula, and Simon," referencing the original *American Idol* judges.

Yes! As he was presenting that idea, I immediately pictured those three people in my life and had to laugh at the mental comparison of Simon to my best friend Judith. Vinny's speech was tailored for the aspiring leaders at the seminar, but the core of his analogy works in our personal lives and for changes as well. Having these personalities in your network so you can seek their insights as you step through change will help make your change as successful as possible.

Randy Jackson was known for calling everyone "dawg" and giving the contestants a metaphorical bad news sandwich. News a contestant was singing completely off key sandwiched between compliments on their outfit and smile always seemed to make for less-teary moments. Your Randy will sugarcoat reality a little for you and is often your tiebreaker if you are stumped on which direction to go in. He will gently push you and will bring a sense of humor every time you feel stuck.

Paula Abdul was the source of compassion and sympathy on the show. She was the one who contestants looked at when they were beyond nervous, and she would build contestants back up if the other judges' critiques left them on the verge of losing their composure. Your Paula is your number one fan no matter how crazy your change path gets! She believes you'll conquer anything in front of you but is also ready to help you pick up the pieces and be a shoulder to cry on if you fall.

Simon Cowell would bluntly tell hopeful stars they couldn't carry a tune in a bucket and needed to not quit their day job to pursue the impossible dream a music career would be for them. You need a Simon. That person, or several people if you're brave, holds you accountable and keeps you grounded in reality. This person asks tough questions, keeps track of your progress, and pushes you onward when doubts arise. They may seem emotionless and cold at times, but they have your best interests in mind.

Be intentional and open about identifying these people in your network. Tell them which role you see them playing in the change you are walking through. This way they know their role and you have clarity about what to expect when you talk to them about your change. Clarity where you can get it is critical in successful personal change because it alleviates some of the uncertainty that makes us want to initially resist change.

Having a solid understanding of who is in your network as you move through life's diverse changes is a foundational piece of the change playbook. It's a big piece, right up there with values, so I wanted to present it in its own chapter. Several other key pieces to the change playbook do not need as much in-depth unpacking but do need addressing. I call these the nuts and bolts, and we'll dive into that mixed bag next.

Coaching Question: Who are your Randy, Paula, and Simon? If you don't have them, where or how might you find these key people in your network?

CHAPTER 9

NUTS, BOLTS, AND COLD HARD CASH

Get the fundamentals down and the
level of everything you do will rise.

—MICHAEL JORDAN

I was on a video call with a fellow author one day when he pointed out it must have been my military experience that had made me consistently see change with a harnessing approach. He definitely had a point. While I was in the Navy, I moved every three years or less and changed jobs about every six months (because you never do just the one job you're trained for in the military—you've always got at least an additional three). There was also the never-ending process of learning new equipment as new technology was introduced to the planes I flew. There was a clipboard hanging in the pilot office spaces that was updated *weekly* with information on anything that had been added to, or removed from, the planes. Constant change for sure.

Learning new towns every three years, making new friends at new bases, figuring out the best route to work, fumbling through new navigation system capabilities in new planes, and so many more connected changes became my way of life. I've been so overly exposed to change that it has become second nature. Until that video conversation with my fellow author, I'd almost forgotten 99 percent of the rest of the population does not move, switch jobs so regularly, or get a new boss every year with same frequency as military members.

This was a giant light bulb moment for me! I hadn't thought of change as a learned skill. I had thought I was innately good at change, that something in my DNA made me able to make changes in my life without hesitation or really thinking about them too hard. I realized after I reflected on my colleague's comment that I wasn't always good at making changes.

I mentioned earlier I grew up in a small town on a barrier island off the coast of Florida. I knew the owners and employees of every quaint shop on our main street from the time I was eight years old to today because they are all the same. It's the type of town where "big change" is renaming a street or adding a new dish to the menu at the burger place that's been open for sixty years. I wasn't exposed to much change in my early years, so change didn't come easy to me until later in life.

I have discovered there are certain basic nuts and bolts fundamentals to the process of change that make it comparable to learning any other repeatable skill set. Every change involves goals, purpose, people, a certain amount of planning, and overcoming obstacles. So far, we have talked about the first three on that list. Those topics are the forest topics. You are zoomed out on the big picture of your change when you are looking at those topics because they encompass every angle. Thinking about those topics first gives you a look at who you will ultimately become (that living room for eighty-year-old you) and the big aim of the change you're making. This chapter is where we'll look closer at individual trees in your personal change forest.

Approach this chapter like an entry-level college course. Here are the base questions and actions you'll need to take to successfully navigate the changes in your life. I'm talking about identifying timelines, financial considerations, conversations to have with people, and other seemingly easy pieces of change. There will be a lot more questions in this chapter than in the previous chapters. Some of the questions may feel a little basic, but that is on purpose. Taking the time to identify the answers to these foundational questions will get your mind ready for the more difficult ones to follow (or that you may have skipped in previous chapters, such as the chapter about values). Knowing what the foundation is made of helps you visualize the rest of the change.

The details in this chapter cannot be neglected. While they aren't necessarily as sexy as discussions about "mindset" and "approach," they are the starting point for any change. They are also the continuing point if you get stuck on your change journey. They are what you fall back on to keep the change moving, much like a layup is an easy point Michael Jordan might have fallen back on when scoring had to happen and there was no room to be flashy.

SKILLS

Everyone brings something to the table. Whether you're applying for school, joining a training program, starting your first job, receiving a promotion, starting a whole new position, rejoining or leaving the workforce, or whatever your change will be, you have something to bring to that arena. Your application, résumé, and verified credentials are part of the package. Those formal pieces of paperwork ask you about your hard skills and skills that are fundamentally applicable to that role. Your ability to type at lightning speed, work any computer program with ease, perform surgery on any animal with one hand tied behind your back, or any number of credentialed and quantifiable skills are your hard skills. These are the minimum items required. Formal paperwork may not be required for your change, but thinking through your hard skills, your "résumé" skills, is still a critical part of making your life change successful.

Think about all of your hard skills as you approach change, even those skills that may not directly relate to the change you are making. I am a certified pilot in many different aircrafts, but that doesn't immediately apply to any of the work I did as a public relations director (PR) for the Okinawa Leadership Seminar (OLS). I might not have put my pilot qualifications on my position application for OLS if my husband hadn't urged me to do so. "It alludes to other skills you have, soft skills," he said.

He was absolutely right. My pilot certification, while not required at all for the PR position, hints at the fact I'm very organized, capable of learning new information very quickly, able to handle *a lot* of stress, and that I have a smooth radio voice perfect for any TV or radio appearances to spread the word about OLS. Soft skills are equally as, if not more, important when making certain changes. Actually, "44% of the executives surveyed [in an Abdecco survey] think Americans are lacking critical soft skills such as communication, creativity, collaboration, critical thinking, etc." (Belcak, 2021).

Soft skills are those skills that don't appear in the unchangeable drop-down menus on most online forms. These skills speak to your unique personality and character. These are the skills that make you memorable: a "go-to" person for something no one can really put a finger on; the person in the office who seems to be the Jack/Jill-of-all-trades; the neighborhood fix-it guru; the best listener of the family. Identifying these skills may also shed some more light on your values that we spoke about previously in Chapter 5. Your soft skills could be anything; not being afraid to talk to anyone, the chili cook-off champion seven years running, or knowing every shortcut on the roads between your house and the highway are some examples that come to mind. These are the skills that truly make you distinctive.

No one is a perfect fit for anything. We all have areas that need improving and developing, even in those arenas we are considered an expert. Being open about these areas with yourself and potentially the leaders in your new role or organization will help propel you to success. If you have a plan to advance those skills, certifications, or education, even better. Make sure that plan is SMART.

Treat any application process, and any skill advancement process involved with the change you are making, as a SMART goal.

Be Specific about what you need to get done. Create a Realistic Timeline utilizing any deadlines you've been given and create your own as necessary. Define Achievement and plan how you will celebrate completion. If you're a master procrastinator, identify someone in your network to hold you to your timeline.

Coaching Questions:

–*What are the formal requirements, if any, for this change? (Application, résumé, interview, test, certificates, school, training, letters of recommendation, other clerical requirements, hard skills, etc.) What are the formal deadlines that accompany those?*

—*What self-imposed, personal deadlines do you need to set to complete the requirements?*

—*What are some hard skills you have that, while not required, set you apart?*

—*What are your top three soft skills?*

—*How have you continued to grow, learn, and develop? Do you go to conferences? Are you a part of any professional organizations? Do you take online courses, participate in related clubs, etc.?*

COLD HARD CASH

While this is not an appropriate dinner party conversation topic, it *is* an appropriate, and *necessary*, topic for any change. Our society does not run on a bartering or deeds system.

Money plays a role, great or small, in most of our personal life changes. Even the unexpected detour in the literal road makes us think about money in the form of gas burned (unless you drive an electric vehicle . . . woosh . . .).

How do you feel about money? I'd never honestly examined my feelings about it before opening my own business and having to ask myself the same question. Some common feelings about money are that it's power, it's safety, it's to be spent, it should be given away to help others, there's never enough of it, or it's fake.

Mark Wahlberg is a popular Hollywood figure associated with dancing on stage in his underwear, while semi rapping, and being generally badass in blockbuster action movies. He's also super money savvy. He told CNBC, "Everybody is about: 'What am I going to do today?' But I think having a long-term plan and strategy is the most important thing you can do [when it comes to money]" (Scipioni, 2019). He's made smart decisions along the way that are aligned with what he cares about, and any risks he has taken were well calculated. Wahlberg examines his finances before diving into anything.

Similarly, you should be examining your finances before any change. No matter if you are single, married, in a long-term committed relationship, the provider for your aging parents, or however your finances are distributed, examining how they will be altered because of the changes you choose is key to making successful change. Have open conversations with those who will be affected financially by those changes, even if they are young children. I'm always surprised at how much children actually understand about the adult world around them. Their little ears hear it all.

Becoming debt free is a goal I hear a lot in my office from clients. When I ask them a seemingly obvious follow up question—"What's your plan to accomplish that?"—I'm often met with confused, blank looks. Becoming debt free is a big change that involves several connected life changes. There are plenty of excellent programs out there to guide you to your debt free goal. The name Dave Ramsey is almost synonymous with this change. His style may not speak to you, and that is absolutely alright, but his website, www.ramseysolutions. com, has some excellent free resources to help you find the right plan for you.

All solid finance plans involve a budget. Think about a change you would like to make. Do you have an effective budget plan to successfully make the change without adding unnecessary debt and stress? Having a detailed, specific budget for your change will remove that element of uncertainty that may be causing you to have a resist mindset about this impending change.

Coaching Questions:

—*Does your current financial state cause you stress? If yes, why?*

—*What does financial success look like to you? How long do you realistically think it will take you to achieve your financial success? Your vision of financial success could be a specific savings number, a specific investment amount, a specific income, multiple*

*real estate investments, or whatever else feels right
and unique to you. Be specific about it and find a
way to measure it.*

*—How does this change get you closer to achieving
your vision of financial success?*

*—What controls are you going to create for yourself so
you adhere to your budget to ensure you remain on
track? Examples of controls might be only paying in
cash for everything, having a very low limit on your
credit card, having a weekly "What did we spend?"
meeting with your significant other or close friend,
and any other creative way you can think of to hold
you to it.*

*—How will you reward yourself for achieving your
financial goals? Like I said before, I always encourage
celebrating life milestones, big or small, in some way.
It brings motivation, it allows you to recognize the
hard work you put into something, and it solidifies
the accomplishment in your mind.*

RESOURCES

Most change is going to require you have, or gain, knowledge
and skills. More often than not, you aren't just born with those
necessary skills or knowledge, and you cannot acquire them
entirely on your own. You cannot go from being a seasonal,
part-time house cleaner one day to a million-dollar cleaning
business owner the next no matter how many people you
know. Kristin Hadeed, the founder and CEO of Student Maid,

tried that approach unsuccessfully. While she was decent at cleaning and pretty good at leading a small group of people, she quickly realized she didn't know the first thing about owning a business. She needed to dig deeper into some resources to launch successfully (Hadeed, 2017). You will have to invest time in identifying and leveraging the resources necessary to make your change.

Depending on if you need more knowledge, skills, community, guidance, or a listening ear, there are plenty of resources ready for you to tap into and fine-tune those elements. Some resources will be traditional and easy to identify (high school, community college, college or university, mentorship programs, faith centers, trade organizations or alumni groups, Rotary clubs—just to suggest a few). Others may be a little out-of-the-box (tourist information centers, agricultural centers or home improvement stores, local historical societies, YMCA, etc.). I recommend you start with your local library because it is its own rich resource and can help you identify other resources you can leverage.

Humor me for a moment and let's try a quick word association exercise. If I were to say the words "Dewey Decimal Classification" to you during casual conversation over some beers, would you know what I'm talking about? I'm willing to bet my next imaginary round of brews that many of you would be at a loss, and that's totally okay. This system has become somewhat antiquated along with its dwelling place—libraries—because of the convenience of the internet. This is unfortunate because libraries, and the staff who operate them, are so much more than just a place where books go to gather mildew on shelves.

Libraries are cultural hubs for their communities. They often have free summer programs for children and adults to learn everything from knot tying to computer coding. They serve as a gathering and meeting place for many local organization boards. Polling stations for elections are often in libraries. Oh, and books on an endless list of topics do live there (including this one). Books, magazines, periodicals, and journals on every topic imaginable are either physically available, digitally downloadable, or the staff can order the resource from another library for you. No matter what your change is, your local library will be a rich resource to draw from.

There is no way for me to know all the resources available to you in your area. There is also no way for me to know all the questions specific to your situation (current or future), but hopefully the questions here will spark other questions in your mind that are unique to you. When this happens, write them down! I like to use the margins of a book, the blank pages in the back of the book, or a journal when questions arise. This keeps the question near the information that caused it to come to mind so I can reference that information later while answering the question.

Taking time to identify the specifics around a change (skills, finances, resources, timelines, conversations to have) is critical for drive and clarity. Whether this is a change you are purposefully making or a change you didn't choose for yourself, identifying the specific facets of this change is vital. It's these specifics that bind us to the mission of the change and help us overcome the inevitable obstacles that rise up along the way.

Coaching Questions:

—*Where are some places you may find information on, or connection to, resources that will aid you in your change? The internet, of course, but think about some of the other examples presented in this chapter.*

—*What groups are you a member of that could connect you with the resources you need? Think groups like alumni associations, faith groups you serve with, places you volunteer with, and other similar places of connection.*

CHAPTER 10

HURDLES

If you find a path with no obstacles, it
probably doesn't lead anywhere.

—FRANK A. CLARK

I asked Katie, "What is holding you back?" Then I patiently waited for her response. It took time. It took probably close to five minutes of silence. Those five minutes were easy for me as a coach because I am used to giving people space to think, but those were hard minutes for Katie.

Katie isn't a client of mine. She's a dear friend who hoped because of my profession I'd help her get moving again on a big life change she was thinking about making. Katie wanted to move to Europe. She dreamed of walking the same Italian streets her art heroes had walked centuries before. She wanted to paint the same scenes that had inspired so many others. She wanted to explore all the museums, attend all the musical performances, and eat all the authentic Italian pasta she could. But obstacles seemed to keep getting in her way. Specifically, *she* kept getting in her way.

When Katie answered my question, she recited a long list of very real fears, reservations, stressors, anxieties, and worries. All of these needed addressing for sure, but none of them warranted the sweat Katie had broken out into on that cool February day. Some of these hurdles would be more difficult to overcome, like the re-homing of her aging cat, but most just required a couple of phone calls or internet research.

"Do you think no one has moved to a foreign country before?" I asked her, mostly to get her to laugh. That backfired because she started to cry and blurted out, "No, I know they have, but I just don't think I can. There's too much stuff in the way." Katie was beginning to self-sabotage.

"The world will put countless obstacles in your path but none will be as big as the ones you create for yourself," says Deep Patel. In his *Entrepreneur* article, he goes on to say "The result of self-sabotage is that we hesitate instead of seizing new challenges. We forgo our dreams and goals. In the end, we know we missed out." Katie reflected on her response to my earlier question after she read Patel's article and was taken aback at exactly how much self-sabotaging she was doing.

No one's path in life is paved in gold, free of speed bumps, and lit by beautiful sunny weather every single day. Stuff *will* get in your way, doubts *will* creep in, and something *will* threaten to keep you from moving forward. If you aren't careful, you'll get stuck and overwhelmed by feeling that the hurdles in your path are insurmountable. This feeling of being overwhelmed will cause you to put your own hurdles in your way, creating a path of self-sabotage like Katie did. I'm here to tell you no problem is too great if you put your mind to it and choose to become deeply determined to progress.

Katie did make the move to Italy a year after our conversation. She dedicated time to methodically overcome every hurdle she foresaw in her path so she could feel confident she was making the right decision. She was sure to get her finances in order, secure a job in Italy that would be flexible enough that she could paint like she dreamed, and took all the steps required for her to bring her aging cat with her so didn't have to leave her friend behind.

The resist mindset is the biggest hurdle to overcome. We've talked about it a lot already. It is almost always a person's immediate reaction to change. Overcoming this mindset is the first hurdle most of us will face. After that, others will arise and the temptation to slide back into resistance will be high. Perseverance, self-discipline, reassessing, and keeping your eye on who you want to become are the keys to conquering the obstacles that arise.

> *Coaching Question: What are your greatest reservations, fears, anxieties, stressors, or worries about this change? Life changes are daunting at any stage— from eight to eighty! Identify these vulnerabilities now so when the associated hurdles arise, you're not surprised.*

PERSEVERANCE

Sang could have easily succumbed to the hurdles in his path. He had the seemingly perfect, comfortable setup in his current situation. He had a fiancée and a high paying job at a company where he was rapidly rising through the ranks. They were living in the city they both loved and were even fortunate to have his parents living nearby. As he began to think about making a change, one of his coworkers created a spreadsheet to demonstrate to Sang how much more money he could make over the next five years if he stayed in his job and continued to promote at his current rate. While the substantial number might be enough to get someone else excited to work hard and keep on that promotion track, Sang still felt like he wanted a change.

Sang took a job at an intelligence agency in Washington, DC, after graduating college. He rose quickly through the rankings until he was a General Schedule Level 14 (GS-14) equivalent (a senior-level manager) before the age of thirty. Due to the high amounts of experience required to be trusted with this level of responsibility, it is almost unheard of for someone as young as Sang to be promoted to that position. But this course was not the position Sang wanted. Sang had always wanted to go to law school and then go on to be involved in politics.

Growing up the son of Korean immigrants, Sang honed his English skills by watching television after school. His favorite show was *The Andy Griffith Show* because the lead actor spoke slowly and deliberately enough for Sang to form the words. Shortly after that show ended in the evening, the news would come on and would often show President Reagan giving presidential addresses. Young Sang thought the Andy

Griffith character and the president were the same person. He was blown away by this awesome human who fought to uphold the law in the daytime and then encouraged others to do the same in the evening. This was Sang's inspiration to become a civil servant and work in politics. He wanted to be part of something greater than himself on behalf of his new country.

This dream of politics stayed with Sang even through his successful career with the intelligence community. Law school was not exactly a requirement to be a politician, but it was highly encouraged. Making the change from his promising, accelerating career to go back to school, and back to the bottom of the workforce ladder, sounded crazy to everyone he told—and occasionally even to himself. Resistance and doubt started to build in Sang's thoughts. Sang told me that "It is still scary every time I think back on it, how if I didn't just kind of close my eyes and jump through the breach, I'd never have done anything I'm doing right now."

Sang leapt over the resist mindset hurdle once he recognized it and the feelings it brought. He left his guaranteed job, moved to a whole different state, and became a full-time student again. Just over a year into his studies, he received a job offer he couldn't refuse, but it meant more hurdles. He took the job and moved back to Washington, DC, where he'd just left a year earlier. To continue law school, he got creative and started night school. This hurdle could have been especially difficult had school not been supported by his new office.

Every time a hurdle arose, Sang found a way to get over it, beginning at a very young age watching evening TV to learn

English. His path to law school and politics was lengthy—it took over a decade to complete—and roundabout, but he wouldn't have done it any other way. He persevered, he got creative, and he kept his eyes on who he wanted to become to prevent self-sabotage. He credits not having a rigid plan for how he was able to handle each hurdle that appeared in his path. "As I get older, I realize it's best not to plan every step or every path. Just plan for the destinations and what one would hope to see in their own life looking back when they are in their final years," he told me after we discussed who he ultimately wants to become. Today Sang is involved in politics, has his law degree, and is on track to become the noble, civil servant his younger self envisioned while watching evening television.

Coaching Question: What needs to happen for you to overcome the hurdle(s) you foresee?

SELF-DISCIPLINE

You may have noticed I am a big sports fan (Geaux Saints!). My dad Jerry, who you met in Chapter 7, coached just about every sport you can think of this side of badminton while I was growing up. His main sport was basketball. His team practices were my after-school care since my mom worked later hours and we didn't live near other family. I spent hours on the gym floor doing my homework but really listening to him push the young men he was coaching. Drill after drill after drill, they would go up and down the court passing, dribbling, shooting, and then repeat it all over and over. At the end of every practice, he would remind them practice didn't stop there. They had to continue to work those skills at home, at night, and on weekends if they were to see any improvements.

My dad could always tell who took the practice at home advice seriously and who didn't. The guys who practiced at home stood out not just because of the physical capability they'd gained, but also their enhanced confidence in their skills. They knew they'd exercised the self-discipline necessary to put in the work to improve and they were ready to show it. One player in particular stood out when he slammed his first dunk. This young man was tall—six feet eleven inches (2.12 m) tall to be exact!

Dunking should have been as natural as breathing for this player, but he just couldn't make the mental connection to gently release the ball through the hoop. He'd slam the ball into the backstop of the basket every time. He put in hours at home for weeks until the day finally came when he felt confident enough to try dunking in front of everyone. He surprised the team one practice when out of nowhere, he flawlessly dunked it! I couldn't believe my eyes at first. I remember jumping to my feet and clapping along with the other players in a thunderous round of applause at his accomplishment.

Self-discipline, when developing physical skills, is an easy analogy to make. You've had to learn a physical skill that took practice at some point in your life. If that skill wasn't dunking a basketball, then maybe it was tying shoes, riding a bike, swimming, or kicking a ball. Developing a physical skill isn't required for every change we make, but almost all changes do involve self-discipline when it comes to time management, organization, prioritizing, and budgeting. I introduced those fundamental skills to you in the previous chapter. Self-discipline to practice these fundamentals in the small changes is how you make them feel like second-nature physical reactions every time you meet a new, larger change.

Coaching Question: Where do you need to increase your self-discipline efforts in your daily life to help you be ready for changes that may come your way?

REASSESS AND CONNECT

Did you notice how in Sang's story he reassessed his change at every hurdle? When leaving his intelligence job, when moving to a different state to be a full-time student, when going back to the first state and starting night school—at each obstacle, he reassessed his decision to ensure he was still aiming for his ultimate vision. It would have been easy to get off course. He could have abandoned the law school dream all together. He could have not taken the surprising job offer and remained enrolled as a full-time student after moving less than a year earlier. He could have easily resisted all the changes that came his way and stayed on the fast-promoting path, but by reassessing, he was able to keep everything in perspective.

My friend Mary went through a similar process when she was going back to school for her master's degree. She had four children and had been a stay-at-home parent for twenty-five years. She knew she wanted to go back to school for an MBA so when she opened her meal prep and delivery business she would be prepared. The first hurdle she encountered during her schooling journey was she became pregnant with their fifth child. "Do I wait even longer or do I dive in and see how far I can get?" was the first question she asked herself to reassess, as she told me during our interview.

Mary decided to charge ahead with her change for as long as she could. She thrived in school for seven months and then realized she really needed to reassess because her due date was coming. With her older children in school, she was determined she could handle it but would need a semester break to dedicate time to her newborn. She picked back up where she'd left off after that break, and life continued to throw more hurdles her way in the form of the passing of a parent, a military move, her husband's extended absence due to a temporary assignment, and several smaller obstacles. She reassessed at every point and worked closely with her school to make sure her needs were met.

While Mary did not complete her degree in the time she had originally planned nor finish with the same school she started, she did complete it. Now, four years and two moves later, she has her meal prep business running smoothly and is confident in her know-how, thanks to sticking with her change. Katie, Mary, and Sang exhibit all three elements required for overcoming hurdles that will arise on your path to change: perseverance, self-discipline, and reassessing.

Change is hard work, and it's never easy. Knowing how to navigate the hurdles is essential to successful change. Knowing how to stick to the changes you've made is equally as important and involves forming habits, which is what we'll be discussing in the next chapter.

> *Coaching Question: Who are you going to reach out to for help overcoming your hurdles? List each hurdle that needs outside help and put the name of a person who can help next to it with the date by which you will reach out to them. The date is important to make the plan SMART (like the goals from Chapter 6).*

PART 3

HOW TO KEEP IT GOING

CHAPTER 11

HABITS

Habit is the intersection of knowledge (what to do), skill (how to do), and desire (want to do).

—STEPHEN R. COVEY

"Great! Go me! That was a really tough change, but dang it, I did it. Now I'm going to celebrate and . . . Wait, now what? How am I going to keep it going?" When we reach the other side of a successful change, I think we all wonder the exact same thing. You used all the recommended skills from the previous chapters to build goals to support your change. Along the way, you networked your little heart out and overcame hurdles to get you to where you are now. You have hopefully been celebrating the successful milestones you have accomplished and the hurdles leaped. So, "Now what?"

Change isn't a one-and-done weekend construction project. You're not making a front door wreath. Change is more like a backyard total redesign that includes adding a pool and deck. You spend months working with contractors for all of the huge items (pool, deck, fire pit, a water feature if you're feeling really adventurous) and you buy just about every plant at the local nursery. You're now the proud owner of a mini orchard of orange, lemon, and lime trees plus an avocado tree so you can rock your breakfast table. There will be pops of color from over a dozen seasonal flowers as well to keep the landscape ever changing. You step back and take a deep breath to admire your hard work.

The problem is that creating this backyard paradise isn't the end of the hard work. Plants need nurturing if they are going to bear fruit this season and into the future. You've got to build the physical habits of watering, pruning, and fertilizing to ensure they continue to grow. If you don't continue to put in the routine hard work for these beautiful plants, frequently reseal the deck, and keep the pool clean, the whole effort will have been wasted.

The same is true for your personal change. You've done hours of hard work up to this point, but if you don't establish ways to reinforce the change, then your efforts will have been wasted. Three ways to lock in changes are through habits, having accountability buddies, and mindfully establishing a legacy. Let's talk about habits first.

PHYSICAL HABITS

Physical habits come to mind the quickest and are the easiest to talk about. You can visualize yourself choosing to do them or choosing not to. I will never take on the Paleo diet lifestyle because I cannot imagine my world without cupcakes. For some people, however, that is a habit they are willing to take on for their weight loss journey. Rebel Wilson made 2020 her year of health and was very transparent about it on all of her social media.

Jennifer Nied wrote a piece on Rebel's transformation in *Women's Health* magazine. In this article, Nied reveals Wilson realized she'd been emotionally eating during the beginning of the pandemic shutdowns. Wilson saw how this could easily spiral out of control and decided to do something about it. She hired a personal trainer who insisted on seven days a week of working out. Then she started a specific diet lifestyle called the Mayr Method. This plan calls for specific food swaps that are unique to each person and altering how you actually eat (like count the number of times you chew each bite!). Another habit Wilson's trainer encouraged her to adopt was taking, and posting, progress pictures as a way to visibly note the changes taking place (Nied, 2021).

Nied noted in the article that "It's easier to make lasting changes to your lifestyle with the mindset that those changes will be long term." That's exactly how Wilson approached her change. She made this a long-term change by adopting physical habits to reinforce the work she was putting in. Wilson's trainer, Jono Castano, had her back in this. He believes change "is never-ending, the journey always continues, so you can never give yourself 10, 12 weeks. Because it just continues, once you reach your goal then what? Then you're going to stop? You can't stop, it becomes a lifestyle you continue" (Nied, 2021).

Habits are how you make your change successful and stand the test of time. If you are working through a weight change, an addiction, or any physical activity change, committing to some physical habits designed to support your change will keep it going. Wilson's example shows how four physical habits helped her cement a change in her life for the long run. When I was trying to get better at shooting foul shots, I searched for drills and practice routines that basketball superstars used to craft my habits to make that change. Find someone who's walked the path of change you want to walk, examine the habits they implemented in their life, and model yours after theirs.

I do not mean you should do exactly what they did because that may not work for you. Wilson favored high intensity interval training (HIIT) workouts for her journey. If you have joint issues or seriously think burpees were designed by a devil for the pure function of torture, then that may not speak to you. Don't let the fact that her exact plan doesn't get you excited stop you from change! Tailor your plan to activities you enjoy that will still get you to where you want to be. If power walking is your jam, do that and get down with your bad self as you work on your lifelong change. "Individuals and habits are all different, and so the specifics of diagnosing and changing the patterns in our lives differ from person to person and behavior to behavior" (Duhigg, 2012).

> *Coaching Question: Who is your change role model? What about that model's change, and the habits they used, do you need to tweak to make them unique to you?*

NOT ALL HABITS ARE PHYSICAL

Habits are also "the prevailing disposition or character of a person's thoughts and feelings" (*Merriam-Webster*, 2021).

Habits are the nurturing processes for the changes we make in our lives. When I have conversations about habits with clients, one of the first books that comes up in the dialog is *The 7 Habits of Highly Successful People* by Stephen R. Covey. I always find that fascinating because the habits he details aren't precisely physical, but my clients are usually looking for easy-to-implement physical habits. We initially seek physical habits because they are easy to talk about and to imagine. More often than not, though, there are also mental habits that have to accompany life changes for them to be successful.

I really did not want to move back to Okinawa, Japan. It's not that Okinawa is a terrible place; in fact, it is one of the most beautiful vacation islands in the world. It's just that we had lived there twice before and we had hoped to go see another corner of the world. I was so against it I broke down in tears when my husband told me that's where his next military assignment would be taking us. I didn't talk to him for almost four days. Admittedly, this was not one of my shining moments. Looking back on this day, I clearly see I fell straight into the enticing trap of the resistance mindset. One minute, I was happily going about my business, and the next I was hit by a Michael Strahan, record-setting tackle from nowhere. Unlike Bret Farve in 2002 when he received Strahan's record-breaking tackle for most sacks in a single season, I did not get right back up.

I pouted. I fought. I complained to anyone who would listen and several people who didn't want to. I made sarcastic remarks to my husband at just about every opportunity and made empty threats to not get on the plane. Not even a month-long road trip through Texas to see close friends and family could get me over the resistance hurdle. By the time I made it to Okinawa, I had firmly set my mind in the habit of being resentful of the Marine Corps, my husband (who really had no say), and the pilot of the plane who took me there for not mysteriously detouring to anyplace else so we never actually made it to Okinawa. I even found myself feeling irritated by every single person who'd said, "Ooooooh, it's beautiful and I'm sure you're going to have an amazing time." This was not a change I wanted, and *the world* had to know.

The pouting continued for close to three months. I lived in sweatpants on my couch in our dark, unadorned, stuck-in-the-1960s base housing living room wrapped in a blanket that still smelled like our beautiful, modern, airy apartment in Washington, DC. Again, not one of my proudest moments. One day a small, optimistic, quiet thought occurred to me. My brain shined a mental spotlight on this thought because it sounded so different from the habitually negative monologue I'd been replaying for three months. "What if you choose to get happy about this?" Say what, little quiet voice? I can *choose* to break my cycle of habitual, negative thinking and *get* happy? Huh?

I wasn't being proactive; I was being one hundred percent reactive. Habit one of Covey's seven habits is to "be proactive" (Covey, 2004). Covey believes being habitually proactive "is about taking responsibility for your life . . . Proactive people recognize that they are "response-able." They don't blame genetics, circumstances, conditions, or conditioning for their behavior. They know they choose their behavior. Reactive people, on the other hand, are often affected by their physical environment. They find external sources to blame for their behavior" (Covey, 2004).

Non-physical habits all start with being proactive about your mindset and mental approach. Change is hard no matter the size or if it was your choice. It's even more difficult if you have the bad mental habit of maintaining a running negative mental monologue around the whole process. I wasted those three months by pouting in my living room cave. I could have been lying on the beach that was a half mile (0.8 km) from my house, scuba diving, island hopping to the smaller outlying islands, or just taking a walk around my neighborhood. My reactive, poor attitude kept me indoors in sweatpants.

Close your eyes. Take a deep breath. Now listen to your inner monologue as you slowly exhale. Examine the tone you just heard. You're looking to determine whether or not your inner monologue needs an attitude adjustment like mine did. Look for outward clues too. If you can't remember the last time you changed T-shirts and you're surrounded by take-out containers, odds are your inner monologue is keeping you in hibernation mode like mine did.

Sometimes our inner voice doesn't even sound like our voice. There are a lot of very vocal influences in your network and in your social media arenas. This can be great if they are a voice of encouragement in your life. I caution you from listening to them too often, though. You want to be sure you are making *your* changes and aiming for the ultimate version of *you* and not the vision they have for you. These influencers clearly want the best for you but their best for you may not be *your* best for you.

The voice you hear mentally surrounding your change can be halting, though, if the person it sounds like is a voice of doubt and judgment in your life. Silencing their voice and focusing on your own will bring clarity to your change process. It will also enable you to take a more active role in your change because their voice was probably holding you back from moving forward.

Take time to search your thoughts for your truest inner voice. Find your quiet, positive inner voice and grab it for dear life like it's a unicorn pool floaty! *Your* proactive, positive voice is your ticket to better mental habits surrounding life changes.

Coaching Questions:

—*Think about what your internal voice has been telling you about change recently. How has your inner voice been cheering you on or holding you back?*

—*What are some of the comments your inner voice has made that have stood out to you, both positive and negative?*

—*Whose voice does your inner voice sound like regarding this change? If it isn't your voice, why do you think this other person is weighing in subconsciously on your decision?*

*—How have you, or how will you, combat the negative
side of your internal voice to ensure your inner voice
is your biggest supporter through this process?*

AND CHANGE AGAIN

It's undeniable once you get the hang of harnessing change
and seeing the positive, successful results that approach brings,
you will resist change less and less. In fact, you may even seek
it out. Military families move a lot more than your typical
American family. Every two to three years, active-duty military members are up for reassignment orders. Those orders
will almost always take the family to a new town, state, or
country. As a result of this, military families have gotten
pretty good at change.

I'm willing to bet if you ask one of my fellow military spouses
what they think about moving so much they will tell you two
seemingly contradictory things: 1) They dread it but 2) They
look forward to it every time. We dread the hassle of packing,
finding a place to live, figuring out schools and neighborhoods,
leaving the friends we've made, and other such details. We
look forward to the new adventures in the new location, the
opportunity to see new sights, try new restaurants, meet new
people, reconnect with friends from previous locations, and
the freshness of all of it. My friend Hilary is no exception to
this seemingly contradictory relationship with military moves.

Hilary's wife, Christina, recently retired from the Marine
Corps after twenty years. Hilary had been with her wife for
eighteen of those years and had moved eight times. Prior to
marrying into the Marine Corps, as we say, Hilary had only

ever moved once, and that was to go to college where she met Christina, and she had never traveled beyond the US borders. Hilary told me the first move terrified her because it took them overseas. The second move excited her because it brought them close to college friends again, and she looked forward to all the subsequent moves for different reasons. She enjoyed all the new experiences that came with each new location and loved to talk about the memories they'd made all around the world.

As they were preparing for Christina's retirement, the question of where they would settle down came up. They both began to feel a bit panicked. The idea of settling in one place took them aback. The three of us discussed where their families lived and if being near either of those locations appealed to them. We also discussed if they'd ever dreamed of living somewhere specific, and we listed several potential "dream" locations. This is when we realized what the heart of the issue was. They'd both grown to look forward to the cyclical changes that came with having to move regularly. That revelation led us to trash the settling down idea and then discuss how they would best like to continue to see the world.

"Willpower, focused attention and mindful action can be used to push through resistance and rewire habitual patterns. This process of intentionally changing our brain circuits is called 'self-directed neuroplasticity'" (Langley, 2021). Hilary had initially been afraid of the constant changes that moving brought. She dreaded the logistics, having to meet new people, and the unknown of a new place. Over time though, she rewired her thought process to look forward to the newness of each move. "If I drive [a truck] down the same track every day that track will get deeper and more open and be easy to drive down while the others will become overgrown with weeds sprouting up through the middle and trees encroaching on the sides. Our neurons work in the same way. The more we drive down one particular path the easier it becomes" (Langley, 2021).

Once you rewire your brain to harness change, you start to see it as an opportunity. Change might even become a habit through map expansion and self-directed neuroplasticity. Hilary and Christina bought a luxury motor coach. They are constantly moving and reinventing themselves when they stop someplace through seasonal jobs. Their goal is to tour all forty nine continental states and all of Canada's provinces in the coach before selling it and picking another continent to tour.

Coaching Question: What changes do you routinely make in your life? What habits are supporting those changes, and how can you apply those habits to other changes you may make?

CHAPTER 12

ACCOUNTABILITY PARTNER

———

It's very important to surround yourself
with people you can learn from.

—REBA MCENTIRE

Leslie knew he had to make a change. He'd known it a dozen times before, and every other time he had failed to make the change stick. "This time would be different," he told himself as he opened the door. "It's lucky number thirteen, so it has to be different somehow at least." The chairs were set up in a circle the same way that they always were. The tired, floral wallpaper straight out of a 1980s department store catalog tried to make the space homey but fell short. The room smelled like a mixture of damp carpet, mediocre coffee, and day-old doughnuts. Leslie saw a few familiar faces and instinctively tried to keep his eyes and head down. They knew he had failed before.

Upon realizing his reflex, Leslie's determined inner voice rallied and alerted him to what was going on. He was falling into the same resistance pattern that had let him down time after time. Leslie was already fearing the change even before it started. It will be hard work. It will change his whole lifestyle. It will fundamentally change him if he does it right, and he'd never hoped to do it right so much before.

This time, number thirteen, was different because he had exhausted all of his chances with the cops, his wife, his parents, and his job. None of their opinions really mattered anymore, though, and the thought of prison no longer scared him. It was the fact he'd exhausted his chances with his kids that brought him back through the doors that night. He couldn't stand how they looked at him anymore. The time for change had come, and he needed it to last.

The leader for the evening started the routine, and Leslie fought his habit of zoning out during the administrative portion. He was waiting for one very important question to be asked, and he couldn't miss his chance. Finally, it came. "Is there anyone here looking for a sponsor?" Leslie shot his hand up before his brain could hold it down. The people in the room who he had recognized upon arriving all smiled at him, and one of them offered to be his sponsor before his hand could fall back to his lap.

"It was just like they say, like a weight had been lifted from me. When I got a sponsor, I knew I was no longer alone. Someone would help and check in on me," Leslie told me during our interview. The missing piece to Leslie successfully kicking his alcohol problem to the curb for good was an accountability partner—a sponsor. Regular check-ins with someone who took an active, invested role in his success and who was going through the same challenge was what this person brought to Leslie's journey. It changed everything.

That night when Leslie got a sponsor was forty three years ago. Leslie hasn't had any alcohol since. "Having a sponsor . . . is a significant predictor of during-treatment and six-month and twelve-month abstinence" according to a 2012 study done by *Addiction* journal. The authors of the study looked at Alcoholics Anonymous (AA) participants who had been attending one, three, five, and seven years. Those who had a sponsor to keep them accountable to their desired change were more likely to attend regular meetings and remain abstinent (Witbrodt et al, 2012).

Having that added sense of accountability was the missing piece for Leslie in his search for lasting change. When the time came, he was more than eager to be that same missing piece for someone else. *"Being* a sponsor is even more important, with sustained sponsorship the best predictor of 10-year abstinence" (Witbrodt et al, 2012). Over his forty three years of sobriety, Leslie has sponsored dozens of others. "I stopped counting at thirteen—seemed appropriate because that was how many times it took for me to stick with the program," he told me with a broad, ironic smile.

Your change doesn't have to be kicking an addiction for the idea of a sponsor to make sense. A sponsor is just AA's specific version of an accountability partner. We talked about the importance of having a Simon in your life back in Chapter 8. Before you get to thinking, "Sarah, we already sort of talked about this when you mentioned how Simon kept tuneless singers from getting through to Hollywood," let's get clear about the difference, and intricacies, between the terms "mentor" and "accountability partner." Sometimes these two terms, and the type of person who typically is one of these, are confused. While similar, they are distinct terms. It's important to understand the difference so you can identify each of these people in your life.

Coaching Question: Who in your life is walking a similar path of change but may be slightly further along?

ACCOUNTABILITY PARTNER VS. MENTOR

June was giddy with excitement when she started her own yoga practice. She had been with a group for three years and was ready to be her own boss. She wanted to finally be able to really focus on the niche clients she wanted to serve most. She told everyone she could think of and then posted it publicly on all of her social media accounts so the world would know too. Some of the very first connections she made were with other self-employed instructors so she could occasionally ask questions of them as she grew her business.

Rachel had been a solo yoga instructor for just over five years when June connected with her. They exchanged phone calls a few times over several months, and June always found their calls insightful. Thanks to Rachel's advice, June chose a website platform, thought about what to charge per individual session, and researched intake forms she needed to create. Ten months after their initial call, June was discouraged and wondering if she'd made a mistake trying to be self-employed. Her website was not live because it only had her contact information on it. She hadn't had any clients despite paying for several ads on various social media sites. Most of all, she was frustrated Rachel hadn't been as involved as she'd hoped.

After a long day of trying to figure out how to optimize the search engine hits on her website (SEO what?), June was frustrated and exhausted. She called Rachel to confront her about her seeming lack of interest. June told me she asked Rachel, "Why aren't you checking in on me and holding me to the things I told you about when we talked last?" Rachel's response was composed and gracious. "June, I thought you wanted mentoring, not accountability."

June confessed to me that until then she didn't think there was a difference between a mentor and an accountability partner. She thought a mentor was someone who would give you advice and help hold you to the promises you made to yourself by actively checking in on you. Rachel helped her to realize that while the difference between the two roles appears slight, it is in fact significant. Rachel explained to June a mentor is like a counselor who's walked in your shoes before but isn't actively walking that path right now. They can give advice based on their own experiences and help you develop your plans for the path you wish to take.

An accountability partner is just that—a partner. You're both working through a similar change on a similar timeline. You actively work to keep each other motivated and on track. It's a mutually beneficial relationship. A mentor-mentee relationship is as well, but in a different way. The mentor benefits from the relationship because the mentee may bring fresh light to something the mentor is working through separately.

You and your accountability partner will help each other set goals, timelines, budgets, and other key elements unique to your own situations. As partners, you push each other to stick to these. Your mentor may ask you about these items, but they do not have any of their own you are helping hold them to. Does Simon Cowell fit the mentor or accountability partner description? A blunt mentor, for sure!

Don't get me wrong. I'm not saying you shouldn't have a mentor. You absolutely should if that relationship makes sense for your particular change. Not all changes need that relationship for the change to endure, but most do need an accountability partner. "The key to success is to find the type of accountability that speaks to a particular style of communication and personality" (Wissmen, 2018). Only you will know what makes the most sense for you and the change you are working through.

> **Coaching Question:** *Have you had one of these two relationships before without intentionally identifying them? How did you find that person if they were not already in your network?*

STEADY, THRIVE, STRIVE

Something beautiful happens when you work closely with others to stay on track. You keep finding ways to support each other long after the initial milestones are met. While June did not use Rachel as an accountability partner, she did take her up on mentorship. The first thing Rachel recommended was June find an accountability partner.

June took that advice and found Chris through a mutual friend. He was just getting started as a solo yoga instructor like Rachel. He was very willing to partner, and share, with someone walking the same path. They mapped out their plans together, shared marketing information they discovered, and checked in on each other regularly. They both now, four years later, have steady and thriving practices.

It wasn't easy for either of them. Obstacles arose at almost every turn. "It cost way more than I anticipated, and I was ready to give up several times. I probably would have had it not been for Chris who was experiencing it, too," June told me in our interview. She also told me their partnership has grown so much from its inception.

Chris and June's partnership was initially made to keep each other meeting a set of identified milestones for their businesses. Now it includes some more traditional business partnership elements such as covering clients for each other when necessary, giving name recommendations if a good fit client is found, looking for and sharing education opportunities that come up, and much more. They are also looking at future business growth plans to strive for. They each would like to have physical locations rather than continuing to work out of client homes. Together, they are formulating their plans to grow their businesses by co-owning a space.

"No successful change is made alone," I said back in Chapter 8 about networking. Having those people in your life who will "tell you like it is" and push you toward your desired changes beyond your comfort zones is critical. Without them, we are less likely to take on change and if we do, it is less likely to endure. Think about the gym on January 2nd. Packed, right? How about on February 1st? Not so much, except for the people who hired a personal trainer or have a regular workout partner. Accountability is key to lasting, successful personal change.

> *Coaching Question: How do you want your account-ability partner to hold you accountable to your change? Be specific! How do you want your partner to challenge you, help you push your boundaries, and help you think big through this process?*

BOTTOM LINE: TEAMWORK MAKES THE DREAM WORK

"The world is so complex, no one person has the skills or knowledge to accomplish all that we want to accomplish," said Susan McDaniel, PhD, a psychologist at the University of Rochester Medical Center in an article by Kristen Weir for *Monitor on Psychology.* Your accountability partner, mentor, and other network connections you identified along the way are your team members. These team members will have the missing knowledge, skills, and motivation to help you through this complex world of change.

Hurdles and obstacles present themselves all throughout any change. You're armed with ways to overcome them on your own, but having a partner or team can make the overcoming that much less painful. "Team players can tolerate twice as much pain as those who work alone . . . Researchers at Oxford

University found that members of its rowing team had a greater pain threshold after training together than when they performed the same exercises individually" (Sample, 2009).

A rowing team is such an excellent example of accountability and teamwork. The rowers have to keep the same pace as those they are partnered with in the boat, or the boat becomes a tippy, lopsided mess doomed to capsize or quit. Chris did this for June. When she felt like she was ready to give up her self-employment journey, he was there with her to take up the oar and pull her through because he was going through it too.

Leslie and June both mentioned during our interviews how much it meant to them that they had partners. They were both sure to routinely thank their partners either verbally or via small acts of gratitude. "I took my sponsor several things I'd whipped up on my grill or smoker. I'm no longer totally sure if he stuck with me because of our partnership or because of my cooking. Guess I'll ask him in the afterlife," Leslie joked.

Showing gratitude to your team as you work through change is essential, not just for making the change successful but for nurturing the relationship so it endures and continues to be mutually beneficial. We've all had that friend who never returned calls, didn't send birthday gifts (let alone a card), and seemed to take the friendship for granted by their lack of involvement. Do you still call them a friend? That behavior will quickly dissolve any partnership.

You don't have to go all Oprah and give everyone a car. Dough-nuts will do, or even a sincere thank you. These people are helping you create a legacy of change success. They have earned some form of thanks.

Coaching Questions:

—*How will you show your accountability partner and/ or mentor gratitude?*

—*In what ways can you be sure to support your partner so the relationship is a two-way street?*

CHAPTER 13

LEGACY

———

*What you leave behind is not what is
engraved in stone monuments, but what
is woven into the lives of others.*

—PERICLES

The big, hazel eyes of my barely six-months-old baby
girl, Emma, observed everything. I also watched as the
packing crew bubble-wrapped photographs, jars of foreign coins, paintings, small statues, and dozens of other
items from our living room marking changes I had made
throughout my life. The US Navy and US Marine Corps
had afforded me the opportunity to live in four states
and Japan through seven moves over the course of the
thirteen years I had so far been a part of their organizations. Each location was an onion of change. The layers
of changes were all interconnected and all needed their
own dedicated attention. This reflection got me thinking,
How will Emma face changes?

I watched as the crew packed a picture taken on the day I earned my "wings of gold"—my Navy Pilot wings. Three of my best friends are by my side in the picture, all of us smiling ear to ear. I was the first of us to earn my wings. That day marked a major change in my life. I was no longer a student. I was now a fully qualified pilot who would be entrusted with the lives of crew members and with the education, eventually, of new pilots in training. Up until that day, I had been solely responsible for my own progress. I had no crew to lead, and I was the one in training seeking the help of others. This change was the final culmination of years of hard work, and that picture captures all of the emotions perfectly in my broad, tear-filled smile.

A plaque from my final duty station with the US Navy—the White House—was next up to get bubble-wrapped. It has the dates I was assigned there etched into it. August 14, 2018, was my final day at the White House and in the US Navy. That was the day I started over. For the first time in just over ten years, I had no job. I had no boss, crew, peers, schedule, uniform, or future assignment. This change was a nearly blank slate. I'd known the day was coming for years, and I had been working the steps to ensure I harnessed this opportunity to the best of my ability. I'd earned a master's degree, trained with an accredited coaching institution, and I'd done a lot of research on business ownership, so I felt comfortable on my new path. Still, starting over was a huge change.

Packing day rushed by in a sea of brown paper, bubble wrap, boxes, tape, and itemized lists of contents that needed my signature. Throughout the day, I reflected on a ton of changes (literally a ton because that's how much all of our boxes weighed). Each one was unique. Not all of my changes were handled well, not all of them were planned, but I did learn from all of them. Emma is my most recent big change. She doesn't yet know the stories behind all of the items, but I will tell her one day because we are responsible for teaching the next generation how to harness change.

MUDPIES AND BUTTERFLIES

I truly believe change is a learned skill. Through the stories of my family, friends, and community, I've shown you fundamental components that make change a skill: setting goals, networking, knowing what your values are, taking an active role, and overcoming hurdles. I've asked you about *who* you want to be when you're eighty. What memorabilia items do you want to have in your living room to remind you of the changes you've made in your life? How do these items and the changes they represent reflect who you are?

Now, how do you set up someone else's living room? Who represents the next generation in your life like Emma does in mine? How will you teach them not to immediately choose a resistance mindset when change comes their way?

In the American South, there's something we call "front porch sitting." That is when a grandma, grandpa, great auntie, great uncle, or other community elders sit with the little ones and recount stories about their lives. It doesn't have to take place on a front porch. The storytelling could happen anywhere: car ride, playground, or a kitchen over a batch of cookies. The stories are what matter. They are stories about how the elders overcame whatever obstacles were in their way or how they took on different changes the world brought to their doorstep. The stories tell how they ultimately became the person sitting in front of the young ones on that front porch.

That's where we can learn the skills of change. That's when we should be teaching each other not to fear change. That's when we should learn to have a growth mindset, not when you're leaving high school or college or joining the job force or getting out of it or when you're in a midlife crisis and you're stuck. We should be learning about the skills of change when we are making mudpies and watching butterflies.

I remember when I was twelve (past the mudpie years, thank goodness) and I needed to make a change. I had been a member of our school band, playing the alto saxophone for two years, and I had been riding horses on the weekends. The horse scene was starting to get more serious for me. I began participating in shows, asking my parents for all the fancy equipment required for that, and began riding on weekday evenings, too. I really enjoyed the band and was doing well there, but horses were where my excitement lived.

I asked my parents what I should do. They didn't tell me which activity to choose. They said that choice was mine alone to make. I ultimately decided to leave the band. My parents guided me through the reflection process, goal setting, and networking so I could secure car rides with friends to the barn since I was a bit too young to drive and both of my parents worked.

My parents also coached me on how to politely leave the band so I did not just disappear from my place one day. Change is an end as well as a beginning, most times. You must take care to handle both sides for it to be truly successful. Horses are still a part of my life, and I look for opportunities to mount up on just about every vacation. The way my parents taught my twelve-year-old self how to successfully make changes has been a model I've pulled from time and time again, especially the skill of polite exits. These skills of change are part of the legacy they will leave me with.

TEACHING THE WORLD

The television show *New Amsterdam* is about a fictional hospital in New York led by medical director Max Goodwin. Max is always trying to make changes. He tries to change policies, processes, approaches—anything to make the patients' experience at the hospital better. In one episode, Max attempts to make some changes to the hospital that will help minimize its carbon footprint (Slovis, 2021). He meets resistance at every attempt. The food he tries to add to the menu is accused of being cardboard, the radiology department rejects his move to limit their rubber glove usage, and the emergency room loathes the time of day he chooses to swap the old light bulbs for more efficient ones.

Max calls a meeting of the staff to address all the resistance he is facing. "The time will never be right, convenient, or easy for change to start," he tells them (Slovis, 2021). The scene cuts, and the rest of the show is spent showing mini scenes of staff members and patients supporting his change efforts—albeit some of them still looking a bit annoyed.

Max is so right! Rarely will change come when you're thinking, "Golly, now would be a perfect time to flip my world upside down." More often than not, it will come when you are happy with your status quo and comfortable knowing your role. The last thing you'll be wanting to do in that situation is make a change.

Having honed the skills of change through mindfully making personal changes, you will be prepared for the unexpected moment when the larger need arises. When your community opens a new homeless shelter and they are looking for advocates and volunteers, you'll be ready to step up. When a natural disaster strikes your area and everyone has to rebuild, you could organize the pooling of resources so no one goes without. When a global pandemic strikes and the restaurants, public transpiration, hotels, and all places of social gathering close, you'll there shouting encouragements to everyone affected in your network. When your children are forced to be home-schooled and life as you knew it alters at its core, you research every creative lesson plan you can so they don't miss beat in their education. Having a skill set for change is what will get you through those times and make you a natural fit to lead those around you who do not have those skills.

After times like those, a mark will be left on your life that will undoubtedly be reflected in a physical way. It may be a new house after rebuilding from the natural disaster, a new business after yours closed during a pandemic, a picture from a grand opening event at the homeless shelter, or any other token that causes you to pause and reflect as your years continue. These are the "living room" items marking milestone changes you will acquire along your journey experiencing and learning how to change.

VALUABLE HAPPINESS AWARENESS

Jasmine's mother knew even before Jasmine did that her living room was the whole world. She knew Jasmine would be a lifelong explorer. "Once I left home, I called my mom to tell her I wouldn't come back and I wanted to keep traveling. She told me she knew. Mothers just know," Jasmine told me over coffee one day. "I started traveling right after university, thinking I would come back to a career. To my surprise, traveling was my career."

Every change Jasmine has made since her initial choice to leave home has kept her aligned with who she is and the value she places on adventure. She's lived in multiple countries and worked in many different roles because she sees each move as an opportunity to change her approach to life. I met Jasmine in Japan when I began taking yoga classes from her. In that one class, she taught in three different languages.

When I asked Jasmine to describe her vision for her living room when she's eighty, she gave me one of the most interesting answers. "My room would be quite bare. I can see plants, books, and chairs on the balcony. The more I travel, the fewer things I need. I still need green and the outdoors." She envisions a nearly empty living room, not because she doesn't have values or goals but because the journey is her goal. She doesn't envision being tied to things or to one place. Not having physical ties to one place so she can be free to change at a moment's notice is how Jasmine chooses to honor the value she puts on her happiness.

Not all change is driven by career, obligation, or social expectations. Some change is driven by your deep internal need to stay true to your values in the most joyful way you can. This type of fluid lifestyle can come with challenges. Jasmine knows some of her relationships have suffered or been lost because of her path. "I met someone, and we were together for a year until a friend asked me to go to Australia for three months. I couldn't refuse, and, well, my partner didn't take it lightly . . . so that was the end of that."

While Jasmine was visibly saddened by that reflection, she is not regretful because she chooses to honor her values every day through every change. Asking yourself the deep searching questions to determine if the change you're facing keeps you true to your values is what will keep you on course to the vision you have of your eighty-year-old self. Jasmine closed out our interview with this insightful statement: "I left as an adventurer. I wanted to see more, to see different lifestyles . . . After a while, I understood it's my life, my path. It's where I feel most comfortable. I'm home everywhere I go, every change I make."

WHAT NOW?

Back in the introduction, I mentioned doing an internet search for "What do people think about change." I hope you did that and saw the returns are largely corporate focused, tips and tricks to changing behaviors, and negative "Why" articles about people resisting change. The negativity and impersonal, corporate angle are alienating. The vast majority of people want to have a positive experience with their change. These people don't see their situation reflected in many of the search returns. You may be one of these people.

My experiences making so many life changes while on active duty with the US Navy and now my experiences guiding people through their life changes as a life and leadership coach prompted me to write this book. Change is something we all do at every phase of life. It's not always about behaviors, or our job, and it's definitely not always a negative experience. Change is a skill, one you hone over a lifetime so you are prepared when new opportunities arise.

It starts by having the right mindset. Understanding the difference between a growth mindset to harness opportunity and a fixed mindset with resistance at its core is step number one. Once you've got that down, it's time to dive into knowing who you are and who you want to ultimately become (sitting in your living room when you're over eighty). Then you must take an active role to make this change successful. Setting goals, networking, examining your finances, having tough conversations with others who are involved with your change, and identifying the inevitable hurdles that will litter your path are the next steps that make up the fundamentals of the change skill set.

Think about those in your life who have set examples for you on how to change. Most of the people in these pages are regular people from my life who have shown me how to successfully make change. They are relatable, everyday people who have sharpened their change skill set over time. Hearing and reliving the stories of these people in my life while writing this book energized me! Stories of people harnessing the opportunities presented in changes they made in their lives get me excited thinking about all the changes coming my way.

In the face of an international move, it would be easy to resist change. It would be easy to see all the potential negatives, but instead, I am humming with excitement from their stories as I set my goals, identify my skills, and work my network to make this change my most successful one yet. You have people in your life with energizing stories as well. Draw from their stories as you hone your skills.

Change is life focusing. If you have the idea of where you want to go and who you want to ultimately become, then every change along the way brings you closer to that person. Change isn't typically drastic. Some might be; you might get a moment like Rebekah Gregory (the woman I mentioned in chapter three who lost her leg in the Boston Marathon bombing). That's a drastic life change no one saw coming! Gregory made it through because knew who she wanted to become and she focused on that ultimate reality.

You can do the same as changes of all sizes come your way. Keep your focus on where you're going, what stories you want to tell the next generation, and what experiences you want to have. Change is no longer scary when you take this approach to it. Change is now an opportunity. You just have to see it that way.

What now? Now you get to work! Whether you are currently working through a change or wanting to prepare for the inevitable changes that will come your way, now is the time to take the components from this book and use them daily for the small changes. Next time your GPS says the dreaded phrase "recalculating," work through the process so when a big change comes, you're practiced.

Also, think about what you are teaching others through your actions surrounding change. Are you perpetuating the negativity, or are you setting a desirable example? Finally, how can you help the world to approach change from a growth mindset? As my friend Saibatu, whom you met in Chapter 2, says, "How you affect change is looking at reality differently . . . It starts at home, then it goes to your neighbor, then it goes to your street then to your community." Change starts with you.

BLANK PAGES FOR YOU TO BRAINSTORM

———

Hiring Heroes

_____

_____

_____

_____

_____

_____

_____

_____

ACKNOWLEDGMENTS

Any worthwhile thing I've ever done has involved tireless effort from my entire community. Without all of you supporting me, encouraging me, and telling me "Quitting isn't an option because someone needs to hear this," this book would have never been completed. The sheer amount of huge life changes I had going on while, ironically, writing a book on change was an ultra-marathon's worth of hurdles we leapt together.

Thank you, Jason. You are my partner, my husband, and my rock. You kept this whole project on the rails through all the trials and Emma-isms that should have derailed it. Your conviction that not only would it get done but it would touch lives kept me going back to my computer every day.

Thank you, Mom and Dad. You've been there since my day one cheering me on in your own unique ways. The support you both gave breathed life into this dream.

Thank you, Judith. You are the other side of my coin, the drama to my llama, and the best friend anyone could ever ask for. Thank you for being my Simon, Paula, and Randy, depending on what the situation calls for.

Thank you to my publisher, New Degree Press, for making this book possible. Thank you, Ty Pinkins, for introducing me to Eric Koester and getting the ball rolling. Thank you to Rachel Mensch, Jacques Moolman, and Abbey Murphy for the keen editing. Thank you, Samuel Dillow and Shysel Granados, for being my accountability partners throughout the cohort. Thank you to Brian Bies, Gjorgji Pejkovski, Nikola Tikoski, and everyone else on the New Degree Press team who helped me along this journey.

Last, but certainly not least, thank you to everyone who supported me by either being interviewed or for purchasing my book during the presale. Those initial contributors include: Jennifer Hlad, Camerone and Eric Carter, Heather Jackson, Alyssa Norris, Hamad Husainy, John Balbi, Breanna Rivera, Megan Dooner, Tara McGrath, Heather Sifuentes, Jennifer Eberly, Veronica Mulherin, Holly West, Christina Hunter, Mona Sims, Stephanie Mafrici, Harriet and Michael Carter, Erin Coatney, Jonathan Gardner, Emily Gyimah, Kay Een, Marilynne White, Michael Kraeuter, Dung J. Duong, Robert Myrick, Robert Harris, James Wade, Mo Garcia, Koyu Parker, Maria Quinn, Wayne M. Bacon, Sarah Mavrak, Spencer Zeigler, Michael Choe, Adam Polite, Maria Segura, Kelsey Barrion, Douglas Smith, Greg Keller, David Johnson, Jesse and Jimmy Mastrom, Susan Hofstetter, Caryn Balmat, Karla Hardwick, Evan Troop, Jake and Nicole Jones, Jessie Brenton, the Stone Family, Achala Dennison, Janelle Voisine, Faisal Elkantar, William Yetman, Kaelin Peterson, Lushan Hannah, Kristin Stephens, Ryan Nichols, Nicholas H. Elliott, Bradford

Webster, Joe Laclede, Tiffany Harris, Kevin Soeder, Aramata and Ismael Bamba, Brittany Vankirk, Leann Oatman, Satsuki Fraling, Thomas Bruno, William Mahoney, Savannah and Derek Jones, Travis Hanebrink, Brandon Weiss, Misty Minton, and Teresa Schade.

APPENDIX

INTRODUCTION

Merriam-Webster. s.v. "change." Accessed May 27, 2021.
https://www.merriam-webster.com/dictionary/change.

Murphy, Mark. "The Big Reason Why Some People Are Terrified of Change (While
Others Love It)." *Forbes*. Forbes Magazine, August 15, 2016.
https://www.forbes.com/sites/markmurphy/2016/08/14/the-big-reason-why-some-
people-are-terrified-of-change-while-others-love-it/?sh=296aada42f63.

CHAPTER 1

Alexander, Erika. "Famous Fried Eggs: Students Debate Effectiveness, Accuracy of Well-
Known Anti-Drug Commercial." *CNNfyi*. Cable News Network, December 6, 2000.
http://edition.cnn.com/fyi/interactive/news/brain/brain.on.drugs.html.

Andersen, Erika. "Why Change Is So Hard (and What to Do about It)." *Forbes*.
Forbes Magazine, September 18, 2019.
https://www.forbes.com/sites/erikaandersen/2019/09/17/why-change-is-so-hard-
and-what-to-do-about-it/?sh=165459353e0a.

Blom, Tonja & Viljoen, Rica. "Human Reactions to Change." Paper presented at the
IAABR/ Academic OASIS—Palm Beach International Academic Conference 2016.
https://www.researchgate.net/publication/308748433_HUMAN_REACTIONS_
TO_CHANGE.

Carbone, Nick. "The New New Coke? Coca-Cola Ditches White Cans After One
Month." *Time*. Time, December 2, 2011.
https://newsfeed.time.com/2011/12/02/the-new-new-coke-coca-cola-ditches-white-
cans-after-one-month/.

Derler, Andrea, and Jennifer Ray. "Why Change Is So Hard—and How to Deal
With It." *Your Brain at Work: NLI's Blog for All Things Neuroleadership* (blog).
NeuroLeadership Institute, December 12, 2019. Accessed May 27, 2020.
https://neuroleadership.com/your-brain-at-work/growth-mindset-deal-with-change.

"Understanding the Stress Response: Chronic Activation of This Survival Mechanism Impairs Health." *Harvard Health.* Harvard Health Publishing, July 6, 2020. https://www.health.harvard.edu/staying-healthy/understanding-the-stress-response.

CHAPTER 2

Dweck, Carol S. *Mindset: The New Psychology of Success.* New York, NY: Random House, 2016.

Dweck, Carol. "What Having a 'Growth Mindset' Actually Means." *Harvard Business Review.* January 13, 2016. https://hbr.org/2016/01/what-having-a-growth-mindset-actually-means.

Grafman, Jordan. "Conceptualizing Functional Neuroplasticity." *Journal of Communication Disorders,* 33(4) (2000): 345–356.

Manz, Charles C. *Power of Failure: 27 Ways to Turn Life's Setbacks into Success.* Oakland, CA: Berrett-Koehler Publishers, 2002.

CHAPTER 3

Gregory, Rebekah. *Taking My Life Back: My Story of Faith, Determination, and Surviving the Boston Marathon Bombing.* Grand Rapids, MI: Flemming H Revell, 2018.

Salo, Jackie. "2020 Events: Yep, These Things All Happened in the Year from Hell." *New York Post.* December 31, 2020. https://nypost.com/list/major-2020-events/.

CHAPTER 4

De Palma, Brian, dir. *Carrie.* 1976; Santa Paula, CA: Red Bank Films. Videocassette (VHS).

LaMorte, Wayne W. "Diffusion of Innovation Theory," September 9, 2019. https://sphweb.bumc.bu.edu/otlt/mph-modules/sb/behavioralchangetheories/behavioralchangetheories4.html.

Ng, Deborah. "How Long Does It Take to Be a Neurosurgeon?" Career Trend. Leaf Group Ltd., August 26, 2019. https://careertrend.com/info-7757196-long-neurosurgeon.html.

CHAPTER 5

Clear, James. "Core Values List." James Clear, June 12, 2018. Accessed May 19, 2020. https://jamesclear.com/core-values.

CHAPTER 6

Doran, G.T. (1981) There's a S.M.A.R.T. Way to Write Management's Goals and Objectives. Management Review (AMA FORUM) 70 (11): 35–36.

Fogg, BJ. "How You Can Use the Power of Celebration to Make New Habits Stick." BJ Fogg. January 6, 2020. Accessed May 21, 2020. https://ideas.ted.com/how-you-can-use-the-power-of-celebration-to-make-new-habits-stick/

CHAPTER 7

Ammer, Christine. *The American Heritage Dictionary of Idioms*. Boston, MA: Houghton Mifflin Harcourt Publishing, 1997.

Grant, Adam. "Stop Asking Kids What They Want to Be When They Grow Up." *New York Times*. April 2, 2019. https://www.nytimes.com/2019/04/01/smarter-living/stop-asking-kids-what-they-want-to-be-when-they-grow-up.html.

Hicks, Robert. "Dealing with Rebellious Resistance." *Physician Leadership Journal*, 2020, 70–71. https://physicianleaders.org.

Merriam-Webster. s.v. "change." Accessed May 27, 2021. https://www.merriam-webster.com/dictionary/change.

CHAPTER 8

The Cambridge Dictionary. s.v. "app (n.) networking." Accessed May 30, 2021. https://dictionary.cambridge.org/dictionary/english/networking

CHAPTER 9

Belcak, Austin. "Soft Skills Employers Want in 2021." *Cultivated Culture* (blog). August 6, 2021. https://cultivatedculture.com/soft-skills/.

Hadeed, Kristen. *Permission to Screw up: How I Learned to Lead by Doing (Almost) Everything Wrong*. New York, NY: Penguin Random House LLC, 2017.

Scipioni, Jade. "The Money Advice Mark Wahlberg Would Give His Younger Self." *CNBC*. July 25, 2019. https://www.cnbc.com/2019/07/25/money-advice-mark-wahlberg-would-give-his-younger-self.html.

CHAPTER 10

Patel, Deep. "8 Ways to Stop Self-Sabotaging Your Success." *Entrepreneur*. December 17, 2018. https://www.entrepreneur.com/article/324900.

CHAPTER 11

Covey, Stephen R. *The 7 Habits of Highly Effective People: Powerful Lessons in Personal Change*. New York, NY: Simon & Schuster, 2004.

Duhigg, Charles. *The Power of Habit: Why We Do What We Do in Life and Business*. New York, NY: Random House, 2012.

Langley, Sue. *Neuroscience of Change: Why Change Is Difficult and What Makes It Easier*. Australia: Langley Group, 2021.

Merriam-Webster. s.v. "app (n.) habit." Accessed May 29, 2021. https://www.merriam-webster.com/dictionary/habit.

Nied, Jennifer. "Rebel Wilson's Weight-Loss Is Due to Exercise, Mayr Method Diet Amidst Her 'Year Of Health' In 2020." *Women's Health*. June 1, 2021. https://www.womenshealthmag.com/weight-loss/a30811784/rebel-wilson-weight-loss/.

CHAPTER 12

Sample, Ian. "Working in a Team Increases Human Pain Threshold." *The Guardian*, September 16, 2009. https://www.theguardian.com/science/2009/sep/16/teams-do-better-research-proves.

Weir, Kristen. "What Makes Teams Work? Psychologists Are Pinpointing the Factors That Make Teams Gel—Research That Has Far-Reaching Implications for Health Care, Education, Research, Industry and More." *Monitor on Psychology*. 49, no. 8 (September 2018): 46. https://www.apa.org/monitor/2018/09/cover-teams.

Wissman, Barrett. "An Accountability Partner Makes You Vastly More Likely to Succeed." *Entrepreneur*, March 20, 2018. https://www.entrepreneur.com/article/310062.

Witbrodt, Jane, Lee Kaskutas, Jason Bond, and Kevin Delucchi. "Does Sponsorship Improve Outcomes Above Alcoholics Anonymous Attendance? A latent class growth curve analysis." *Addiction*. 107, 2 (2012): 301–311. https://doi/10.1111/j.1360-0443.2011.03570.x.

CHAPTER 13

Slovis, Michael, dir. *New Amsterdam*. Season 3, episode 11, "Pressure Drop." Aired May 11, 2021, on NBC. https://www.nbc.com/new-amsterdam.